The Diabetic Cookbook

The Diabetic Cookbook

Michael Swamy

BLOOMSBURY
NEW DELHI • LONDON • OXFORD • NEW YORK • SYDNEY

BLOOMSBURY INDIA
Bloomsbury Publishing India Pvt. Ltd
Second Floor, LSC Building No. 4, DDA Complex, Pocket C – 6 & 7,
Vasant Kunj, New Delhi 110070

BLOOMSBURY, BLOOMSBURY INDIA and the Diana logo are
trademarks of Bloomsbury Publishing Plc

First published in India 2021
This edition published 2021

Research: Michael Swamy, Mugdha Savkar & Vipul Sharma
Editing: Tania Bhattacharya
Food Styling & Photography: Michael Swamy

ISBN: PB: 978-93-89351-16-3, eBook: 978-93-89351-18-7

2 4 6 8 10 9 7 5 3 1

Printed and bound in India by Thomson Press India Ltd.

To find out more about our authors and books, visit
www.bloomsbury.com and sign up for our newsletters

Disclaimer: This book has been written keeping in mind a general diabetic audience. It is in no way a book of remedies and readers will still need to follow a prescribed course of treatment by doctors, nutritionists and dieticians qualified on the subject of diabetes. Before following any of the recipes, kindly consult with your doctor or nutritionist if any particular ingredient(s) is not suitable for you at any stage. This book does not provide general medical information or answer questions regarding personal medical conditions. If you have questions about a specific medical condition, please consult a healthcare professional.

For

Suresh Gopal

'The Memories Captured in Each Ray of Light'
You meet people, some stay, some go.
Each one changes the way we see the world and life at large.
The journeys, secrets, memories shared remain forever etched in one's mind.
Some adventures are left incomplete, beautiful in their imperfections
and some have no connection at all to the journeys to come.
All that's to be said is Thank You for leaving behind
beautiful memories for us.

– Michael

CONTENTS

LE CREUSET

INTRODUCTION

A journey is a journey of the senses. One imbibes, one learns and one moves on. Memories of food linger on one's taste buds, memories that are often pressed within the pages of time. It is these recollections that bring to the fore a nature and concept of food and wine, clinging to tell a tale of love, peace and contentment, both physical and emotional. Stories within a plate and journeys often incomplete create mysteries. We all can but get a glimpse of the cuisines of the world and partake of them bit by bit.

Most cuisines are deeply rooted in old traditions and customs and you can taste the mountains, the seas and the plains in the dishes belonging therein. Despite the amalgamation of myriad cultures, cooking styles and techniques, ancient cuisines have retained their connection to their origins and nature to make for heart-warming, nutritionally wholesome and emotionally enriching experiences.

The Health Awareness Centre Mumbai, which set me on a path to holistic food in the tenth grade; Mugdha's mother who reversed her diabetes, giving me proof that it is indeed possible to return to a state of optimal health; the many doctors we met along the way and their expert advice—all of these have inspired me to experiment with food in a way so that it's not only a treat for the senses but also good for our overall health, as well as in the memories it creates. So, whether I'm cooking or dining, my endeavour is to achieve three things—the exotic, the exciting and the new.

—Michael Swamy

HOME COOKING: A WAY OF LIFE

The need of the hour is fine food, but how do we define 'fine food' that is not detrimental to one's health? The rise in lifestyle diseases is heavily upon us. The connect with nature has disappeared with modernisation and urbanisation.

As chefs, we have a responsibility to our guests and what we serve them. The journey of changing one's palate and creating healthier menus without actually calling them healthy is a challenge these days.

Though this book follows the vegan trend, there are also recipes for a paleo diet. There was a time long ago when humans were gatherers and hunters. What consisted as food was a wholesome diet and they ate and grew foods that were natural and of the region. These wholesome foods also made their bodies healthier.

All said and done, there is no right way to eat for all people and generations. The Palaeolithic Age had a variety of foods depending on what was seasonal and what was available. While some had a low-carbohydrate diet, others consumed high amounts of plants with plenty of carbohydrates. But whatever the diet has been, the main foods to avoid are sugars, processed foods, most dairy products, margarine, vegetable oils and trans fats.

While working with resorts in Dhanachuli in the Himalayas, or wildlife resorts in Corbett and with Pugdundee Safaris in Madhya Pradesh, we connect with many staff, who have their own farms, as well as with the properties' gardeners. Out there, in rural areas, food is as rustic as it can get. One is dealing with organic produce at its most basic level. After all, chemicals are only a new introduction to our way of life. Food was always organic and had a different impact on the lifestyle of our grandparents.

Of late, cooking at home has taken on a whole new meaning. People are out shopping for the latest fads, the latest new ingredient or the latest, most expensive food. When we travel, we eat; when we eat, we travel. Food is the epicentre of our moods, our emotions and our memories.

What most have to return to is the cooking of grandmothers and our forefathers. They had knowledge of the seasons and local foods that were good for their bodies and systems. Foods from distant lands did not necessarily mean it suited everyone.

Similarly, knowing the sources of one's food and water is paramount. It's not just about cooking and eating. It's about understanding and experiencing local cuisines and their relationship with their surroundings, and how both food and environment are co-dependent. Our very notion of life is threatened by climate change, and what others thrust upon us.

As chefs, we are given a choice to feed people, as well as create brands and trends. We carry a responsibility to feed regardless of whether a client is paying for a meal or not. As chefs, it's our duty to be responsible about what we serve in our restaurants, or what we advocate when we are grandstanding and talking about safe food, safe food practices and the environment.

What the modern cook or diner needs to know is that talking about food is not just talking about recipes; it's talking about the geographic nature of an ingredient, its seasonality and the changes that happen in one's body during each season.

As a modern generation, we have lost touch with nature and with the farmer. That banter between our grandparents and vendors has all but disappeared in the age of the supermarket, where we take what is being offered with no questions about origins whatsoever.

Today, we are seeing the effects of neglect—mercury and plastic is in almost everything that comes out of the sea. Even sea salt has been affected. The lack of change in farming practices has denuded the earth. What we think of as organic isn't really organic. We read about how high pesticide levels have resulted in greater occurrence of diseases like Alzheimer's and dementia, to name a few. Aluminum and non-stick pots and pans also cause many changes to our system.

Our ancestors had it right—using copper and iron vessels to cook, which are safe. Modernity has affected how we cook and what we cook in. Our forests and ecosystem are being changed for the want of fossil fuels—where will wildlife go and what will happen to the farming world? The natural hierarchy in the wild has been broken with the slow disappearance of the top predator. The disappearance of bees and insects will affect pollination and this, in turn, will affect creation of fruit and vegetables.

There is a change coming in what we eat and drink. But should it be full of chemicals and pesticides? That is the question. As chefs, we need to stand together and question what we are being sold in supermarkets. The right to want what is good for one's body, and one's loved ones, is inalienable.

There's also the question of ingredients we are used to in our diets. If you question how much water is used to grow crops like sugarcane, rice and wheat or to produce meat, you will be amazed. You may stop eating these products immediately! The next war will be over water, so, are we willing to grow foods that need too much water to be produced?

A change in diet is definitely called for in times to come. Eating less seafood and meats is the next step towards food security and sustainability. Foods that travel long distances by way of export and import leave behind a massive carbon footprint. The consumption of government- and business-controlled foods like milk, meat and sugar needs to stop. It is when we stop consuming these products that we can have a culinary impact on climate change. It's not just chefs who can bring about this change but also a large section of home-cooks who are being careful about what they eat.

NEW FOOD

'Our industrialized diet of refined flour, poor-quality fats, and an unbelievable amount of sugar has set the stage for diabesity to thrive.'

—Dr Mark Hyman

Energy, diet, you name it—they all boil down to the kind of food we eat.

'Eating healthy' are the first words that come to mind. Be it at home or at a pub or restaurant, one will have to keep an eye on those calories. Losing weight drastically is not a safe bet. Building up a good exercise regime where you burn fat and not muscle is advisable. Yoga, tai chi, walking and meditation are good options.

Eating less burns up stored fat to supply energy needs, and this can leave you feeling tired and weak. So how does one solve the problem? Well, it's relatively easy. It's just a question of not overdoing it. Too much of a good thing is also not a good thing.

Food comprises three major food groups—carbohydrates, proteins and fats. The fourth and minor group is inorganic salts. Each group is an important factor in the functioning of the body.

Carbohydrates are obtained from starchy foods like grain, fruits, vegetables, sugar and syrups. All these break down into insulin and sugar in the system. So, it is important to remember that if you don't burn up the sugar, it turns into fat. Carbohydrates also play an important role in the release of insulin in the body. The more insulin is let out, the more food gets stored away making you hungry over and over again. Go easy on cereals, cakes, breads, starchy vegetables and bananas.

The second major group is protein. Proteins are made up of amino acids and come mainly from chicken, lamb, cheese, fish, eggs and tofu made from soya beans. Proteins are the building blocks of the system, without which there is loss in muscle mass, lower resistance in the immune system and reduced metabolism. Protein plays an important role in letting your body release a hormone known as glycogen, which helps the body to let go of stored fat, and the liver to release sugar stored in the bloodstream. Proteins help control one's hunger at satisfactory levels and send signals to the brain that the body does not need more carbohydrates. Lean cuts of meat, skinless chicken and duck, tofu and fish are the best sources of protein. Go easy on the cheese for it is high in fat.

Myths around fat swing both ways and leave one confused. However, the body does need some kind of fat. The role of fat in the system is twofold—it indicates satisfaction, thereby, preventing overeating, and slows the digestive process, thus, distancing the time for the next meal. The right type of fat is the monounsaturated variety found in nuts, olive oil and avocados in particular. A tablespoon of nuts makes for a healthy, energy-filled snack.

The fourth food group, though minor, consists of inorganic salts and alkaline foods. The latter are rich in phosphorus, iron and calcium, and the body requires minimal amounts. Vegetables and eggs are rich in calcium; eggs also contain iron along with lean meat, cabbage, string beans, spinach and other greens. Cheese, curd, bananas, cucumber, grapefruit, oranges, peaches, pears and pineapple are rich in phosphorus.

SUPERFOOD

ALOE VERA

Growing up, we had a tiny strip of a garden, which I was paid a rupee a day to water, where there was always an aloe vera plant. Its waxy cactus texture was always a delight to touch. Shakubai, my nanny, would break off a tiny piece and rub its sap over my myriad cuts and bruises at the time—aloe's healing properties are legendary! The plant is also high in antioxidants and its gel-like properties are reconstituted to make it edible. Besides being a unique healing agent, it is known for reducing blood sugar levels. There are many beverages in the market but a lot of them contain added sugars. Read the labels before purchasing any aloe vera-based beverage.

APPLE CIDER VINEGAR

On top of my list for controlling one's diet, apple cider vinegar has been proven to regulate blood sugar and reduce one's craving for carbohydrates. Stir a tablespoon into a glass of water and drink first thing in the morning. Cider vinegar is known to be great for weight loss as well. A few tablespoons of apple cider whisked with olive or coconut oil, seasoning and mild herbs make for great salad dressings. Leave out those synthetic vinegars available in the market. Fruit-based vinegars are great for the system.

BELL PEPPERS

The myriad colours of bell peppers make it an attractive vegetable. From tiny shapes to large ones, these are always on the list of purchases when shopping. These sweet peppers are loaded with vitamins and beta-carotene. Red bell peppers also contain lycopene, which lowers the risk of diabetes. These can be eaten raw or cooked in a variety of ways. One of my favourite methods is to make raw sauces or use them in salads and salsas. Bell peppers can be made spicy or sweet, depending on what varietal one chooses—at the end of the day, it's all about experimentation and using peppers to add colour and brighten up dishes.

BITTER GOURD

A wonderful vegetable whose range of healthy properties is still being discovered, karela is more commonly known as bitter gourd or the Chinese bitter melon and is used widely in Asian cooking. It is also used medicinally. The pith must be removed before cooking. The karela is quite bitter and must be salted to draw out bitter juices. Soak a few slices of karela in warm water and drink it—the juice can help combat cancer and diabetes.

BLUEBERRY AND BILBERRY

I always remember my friend Carolina from Chile whenever I encounter these magical fruits. Chile is the largest exporter of blueberries and we have South America to thank for most of the magical fruits that made it across the world with the migration of the Spaniards. Dried or fresh blueberries are my favourite snack and they also make for wonderful purees, sauces and desserts. What is even better is that its antioxidants fight cancer, and help people with dementia, Alzheimer's and cognitive diseases. Blueberries are full of flavonoids and fibre, which greatly help in insulin sensitivity. In Europe, you get a version of the blueberry called bilberry, which has even higher proportions of anti-inflammatory properties. It also contains anthocyanins, a wholesome antioxidant that strengthens the heart and lowers blood fats.

CARROT

As a kid, carrots were my favourite munchie; I'd sneak away a few pieces from the chopping board while gran prepped a meal. I always got a look of stern fondness when she caught me in the act. Carrots are not just baby food or some vegetable to add to a dish. They're great for fighting cancer, and, growing up, I was always told to eat carrots to good eyesight. I guess they forgot to tell me that it's also great for fighting diabetes. Whether plain or parboiled, in salads or as a vegetable, try and get as many carrots into your system daily, for they contain tonnes of vitamin A. Carrots can regrow if the top is carefully planted, so if you have a green thumb, don't discard the tops.

CINNAMON

The aroma of cinnamon and baking spices around Christmas or in a bakery shop is almost magical. It is always delightful to receive my haul of Sri Lankan cinnamon when my friend, who is always travelling, picks them up for me. The aromas are almost scintillating. Cinnamon has always been my go-to ingredient for anything to do with pastries or when one is in a fix for a magical flavour. This versatile spice and its bark are precious medicinally too. Place a piece of cinnamon under the tongue and keep for a while—it's known to reduce weight as well as blood sugar and is full of powerful antioxidants. Just add a pinch of cinnamon powder to a morning brew or mix it with some honey, lemon and hot water.

COFFEE

Drinking a hot beverage first thing in the morning has many comforts and selecting what to drink can be fun. Many have stopped drinking tea or coffee due to tannins, so that too has been sorted for those who worry—black coffee and cold brew

to the rescue! Coffee is full of antioxidants and green coffee also burns fat. Add a couple of spoons of freshly ground coffee in a tumbler, pour cold water over it and leave it to soak overnight. Strain the coffee through a very fine muslin cloth or a strainer into a fresh cup. The last few dregs will be cloudy so discard them. Add a few cubes of ice and you have your fix of homemade cold brew. If you love your coffee hot, go ahead; just don't add creamer or sugar. Instead, go for vanilla syrup, cinnamon powder, ginger or cold-pressed coconut oil for a unique flavour.

DARK CHOCOLATE

Now, who doesn't love chocolate, except for the small percentage of people who don't or the few who may be allergic? Some of the best cocoa is from South America though the Swiss have perfected the art of making the best chocolate in the world. Dark bitter chocolate or any dessert high in cocoa is rich in flavonoids, which improve insulin sensitivity and reduce fasting blood glucose levels, thus, helping to reduce food cravings. The best results come from chocolate containing 85 per cent or more cocoa. One way to enjoy dark chocolate is to melt it in a microwave oven in short 30-second bursts. Stir as it warms and add a pinch of cinnamon or ginger powder, or, better still, orange or lemon peel. Spread it out on a sheet of butter paper or pour into a chocolate mould, sprinkle with a bit of sea salt or chilli powder and leave it to set.

FISH

No perspective is altogether wrong, and our diets do need to change to save our oceans, depollute our rivers, lakes and seas and let marine life regenerate itself. While I advocate a vegan lifestyle, there are people who want their proteins from meats. I recommend fish like halibut, salmon and tuna, which are rich in Omega 3 and fatty acids. These help regulate blood pressure, keep internal inflammation at bay and fight diseases like dementia and Alzheimer's.

FLAXSEED

This wonder seed is tiny but filled with Omega 3, oxidants and fibre. It doesn't have much to offer by way of flavour but goes well in shakes and pastes used in cooking.

GARLIC

I first tried baking garlic gently, with a bit of olive oil and rosemary, for a few hours during my college years. The flavour of garlic was unmatched until I tried fermenting it into black garlic—which I learned from Roberto Zorzoli, the head chef of Romanos at JW Marriott Mumbai Sahar—and using it. That liquorice flavour enhances my dishes, and I've also grown to understand that garlic is great for treating a multitude of diseases, significantly heart disease and high cholesterol. Kashmiri garlic is medicinal, effective against many ailments and best had raw first thing in the morning. To make black garlic, wrap whole pods in foil and place in an electric rice cooker or a warm oven for 15 days. It ferments and eventually turns black, and the unique flavour goes with just about anything.

GREEN JUICE

A friend of mine, whose mother had restored her health by diligently controlling her diet, introduced me to a blend of spinach, apple and coriander, to be drunk first thing in the morning. It is an excellent concoction for diabetics, and the perfect way to get in all the important nutrients and vitamins from multiple servings of vegetables in one glass!

GREEN TEA

Tea, without fail, restores the spirit and soothes you whatever be the circumstance. A hot cup of tea in the harsh summer heat adjusts body temperatures, while, on a winter's day, works magic for the soul. The camaraderie around tea is almost nostalgic. I was taught by Anamika, a tea sommelier, to never heat water for tea over 90°C and never ever allow it to boil for it deoxygenates the water. Green tea is nothing but the fresh young leaves of the plant, but each tea blend suits different times of the day. Not only does it boost one's metabolism, but its high level of antioxidants is great against diabetes. Matcha supposedly contains 10 times the quantity of flavonoids than regular green tea.

INDIAN GOOSEBERRY

Amla is high in vitamin C, which is found in many citric fruits and is highly beneficial for diabetics. There is a great pickle made in India of raw amla, salt and a few dashes of red chilli powder. Dehydrated amla coated with a blend of spices called chaat masala is available as a snack, or just something to nibble on long journeys.

JAVA PLUM (JAMUN)

Jamun is great for reducing sugar levels. A purple late-summer seasonal fruit, it is made into syrups and vinegars to last the whole year. Also known as the Java plum, its rich dark purple colour comes from anthocyanins in the skin. Besides antioxidants, jamun is rich in vitamins A and C, folic acid, potassium, zinc and iron. The plant extract is used to reduce glycosuria and blood sugar.

LEAFY GREENS

Urban farming and hydroponics are on the rise and people enjoy growing their own leafy vegetables on the terrace or in a garden.

Leafy vegetables not only play an important role in diets; certain nutritious vegetables like spinach and kale, and herbs like methi, which is often used as a vegetable in Indian cooking, aid in healing of the body.

NEEM

Where the neem tree is concerned, each part is useful to the body. High in antioxidants, the leaves, stems and roots are used in Ayurvedic medicine and home remedies. The neem tree is native to India.

NUTS

Come Diwali or festivals, it seems like nuts are everywhere. Varieties like pecans, walnuts and almonds have great health value. Brazil nuts are another favourite of mine and go great with natural desserts and sugar-free foods. Have a few daily to lower blood sugar levels amongst other benefits.

OILS: COCONUT OIL AND EXTRA VIRGIN OLIVE OIL

Coconut and olive oils not only have health benefits but are great to cook with some wonderful ingredients. They are full of antioxidants and suit a high-fat diet, which has been shown to be beneficial for Type 2 diabetes, in comparison to a high-carb diet. However, oil is oil at the end of the day, so use it moderately.

RASPBERRY

Growing up, one of my favourite beverages was a raspberry soda, but slowly I realised, while using them in desserts and such, that its tartness can truly bring balance to creative dishes. High in antioxidants and vitamin C, raspberries are a great alternative to blueberries.

RED ONIONS

Onions are common to most recipes, but do we eat enough? Crushed red onions, onion pickle or onion and chillies make for great meal accompaniments. A simple dish of olives, garlic and herbs tossed with red onion wedges makes for a great starter. What onions have is a combination of flavonoids, foliate, potassium and fibre—excellent to keep diabetes and heart disease in check.

STEEL-CUT OATS

Kids love porridge and as a chef I love adding dried fruits, cinnamon or just a dash of Angostura bitters to the dish. One can add flavoured protein too. Oats porridge is great to warm up the body, and its dietary fibre, an added bonus. Instead of milk, I use water or a bit of fresh juice to cook the oats. It's a nostalgic dish full of childhood memories both good and bad, but either way it's great for diabetics. Besides porridge, you can use oats to make bread, thicken sauces or coat culinary delights like cutlets or croquettes.

TURMERIC

This ritualistic spice is essential to Indian cooking and adding turmeric to foods to fight cancer in other countries that don't traditionally use it is on the rise. It's not a flavour best enjoyed raw, but when cooked, it adds a unique flavour. Like cinnamon, it improves insulin sensitivity and lowers blood sugar levels as well.

YAMS

Yams are on top of the list of superfoods for diabetics due to its nutritive content that also helps control cholesterol and blood related issues. A yam's carbohydrates are different from those of potatoes, contributing to a glycaemic index of 54 against 80 of potatoes. In addition, yams are a source of fibre, vitamins B6 and C and micronutrients like manganese, copper and potassium.

YOGHURT

Milk is harmful for our systems but yoghurt, a by-product of milk, with its good bacteria, can combat harmful bacteria in our bodies. It's great for leaky gut as yoghurt is high in probiotics, calcium, magnesium and vitamin D. A bowl of lightly whisked yoghurt with berries or any other fruit is a delightful combination. It's best had on its own and not as part of a meal. A glassful of lassi with freshly chopped coriander, green chilli and sea salt is a great blend to beat the heat anywhere.

SOUPS

Soups are a great source of nourishment and can go a long way in bringing comfort and restoring health. A good soup is wholesome enough to be a meal on its own!

For a good hearty soup, one only needs to keep some simple tips in mind. Use the freshest ingredients, a good fortified stock for the base and play with flavourings like herbs, spices and flavoured salts. To make your bowl even healthier, substitute flour or cream with thick vegetable purees or pureed lentils for a creamy texture. And remember, don't boil the soup for too long as this will result in loss of nutrients.

SARKI

Cold soups are a class in themselves and, contrary to the popular belief, India is no stranger to them. This cold lentil soup is one of my favourites, and I love eating it in the summer when I visit my Bohri friends. I can spend hours in the kitchen learning their recipes, especially how to make delicious biryanis. But of all the recipes I've learnt, this one remains special because of its refreshing quality. Traditionally, the cucumber is grated and added as garnish. However, in this recipe, I've blended in the cucumber to give the soup more body and flavour.

SERVES 4

¼ cup split pigeon peas (arhar dal)
2 cups vegetable stock or water
1 tsp cumin seeds, lightly roasted
1 cup whisked yoghurt
1 large cucumber, peeled and roughly chopped
2 green chillies
2 spring onion stalks, roughly chopped, plus chopped greens for garnish
Salt to taste
1 cup crushed ice
Juice of 1 lime

Combine lentils with stock or water and cumin and bring to a boil over high heat. Boil until the lentils are tender and mashable, skimming off any scum that rises to the surface. Cool the mixture to room temperature and strain, reserving the broth and lentils separately.

Grind the strained lentils in a blender with yoghurt to a smooth puree.

Add the remaining ingredients (except lime juice) and blend to a smooth puree.

Strain into a bowl and whisk in the remaining broth. Refrigerate to chill. Add the lime juice just before serving.

Garnish the chilled soup with the spring onion greens and serve.

CARROT AND GINGER SOUP

Stacks of carrots with their stalks is a sight that takes me right back to picture books of my childhood. Pulling them fresh out of the ground is an experience I will never forget—simple yet enjoyable! Rich in vitamins, here, the carrot is paired with the soothing qualities of ginger, the wonder herb known to heal many ailments.

SERVES 4

- 2 tbsps rice bran oil
- 1 medium onion, finely chopped
- 4 garlic cloves, finely chopped
- 1 celery stalk, finely chopped
- 1 kg carrots, peeled and roughly chopped
- 2-inch piece of fresh ginger, grated
- 2 tsps cumin powder
- 4–6 cups vegetable stock
- Salt to taste
- ½ to 1 tsp freshly ground black pepper
- 2 tbsps chopped fresh dill, for garnish
- 2 fresh parsley sprigs, chopped, for garnish

Heat the oil in a saucepan over medium heat. Add onion, garlic, celery and carrots and sauté until the onion is translucent.

Add ginger and cumin powder and stir in the stock.

Bring the soup to a boil, lower heat and simmer for 30 minutes, stirring occasionally until the carrots are cooked through.

Cool the mixture and blend into a smooth puree.

Strain the pureed soup into a pan and place over low heat. Add salt and pepper.

Bring the soup to a gentle simmer over low heat.
Garnish with dill and parsley and serve hot.

CURRIED OKRA SOUP

Okra may not be a global favourite because of its slimy texture, but it is a wonder ingredient for those who need to control their blood sugar. My mother, a serious diabetic, had been prescribed half a glass of okra water every morning, which she drank with the biggest frown on her face. We tried this simplified version of gumbo one day and she never frowned again.

SERVES 2–3

1 cup baby okra
2 tsps vegetable oil
1 tsp cumin seeds
1-inch piece of ginger, finely grated
1 medium onion, finely chopped
1 tbsp curry powder
6 cups vegetable stock or water
½ tsp salt
½ tsp freshly ground black pepper
Juice of 2 limes
A few fresh parsley sprigs, chopped

Wash and dry the baby okra and slice off the tops and tips.

Heat oil in a heavy saucepan over medium–low heat and add cumin and ginger. Sauté for a few seconds till fragrant.

Add onion, curry powder and okra and sauté until the okra is tender.

Stir in stock with salt and pepper and bring the soup to a simmer for 5–7 minutes.

Remove the pan and stir in lime juice. Garnish with chopped parsley and serve hot.

AJWAIN TAMBULI

South India can be scorching in the summers and this soup is the perfect antidote to the unforgiving heat. Made from simple ingredients like coconut and buttermilk, it comes together with the anti-inflammatory carom leaves to make for a refreshing and soothing drink before lunch on a hot summer afternoon.

SERVES 4

- 1 tbsp vegetable oil
- ½ tsp cumin seeds
- ½ tsp coarsely ground black pepper
- 8 large fresh carom leaves, washed, pat dried and finely chopped
- 3 tbsps grated fresh coconut
- 3 cups buttermilk, slightly sour
- Salt to taste
- ½ tsp black mustard seeds
- ¼ tsp asafoetida
- 2 dry red chillies, broken into pieces
- 1 small sprig of fresh curry leaves

Heat 1 tsp oil in a frying pan over medium heat and add cumin seeds and pepper.

When the cumin crackles, add the carom leaves and sauté until they wilt and release some moisture. Remove from flame and cool to room temperature.

Blend the carom leaves with the grated coconut and ¼ cup buttermilk into a smooth paste. Then add another cup of buttermilk and blend until smooth again.

Mix the puree in a bowl with remaining buttermilk, add salt and stir well.

For the tempering, heat the remaining oil in a small pan over medium heat and add mustard seeds, asafoetida, red chillies and curry leaves. When the spices are crackling, pour the mixture over the prepared tambuli.

Serve immediately.

TIP

This soup can also be prepared by substituting carom leaves with spinach or amaranth.

BONDA SOUP

When you're on a train journey, there's nothing more exciting than fried bondas or dumplings at railway stations. Dunking them in railway tomato soup was a fun pastime during long journeys. Who would have thought that the combination of a soup and the versatile bonda would capture the imagination of a creative chef to cater to ravenous after-college appetites? Here, the bondas soak in the goodness of a lip-smacking lentil broth, making this a complete meal in itself.

SERVES 4

Dumplings

1 cup split white lentils (urad dal), soaked overnight
2 large green chillies, roughly chopped
½ tsp cumin seeds
Water as needed
Salt to taste
1 tbsp semolina
Oil for deep frying

Soup

¾ cup split pigeon peas (arhar dal)
4 cups vegetable stock or water
½ tsp turmeric powder
A pinch of asafoetida
1 tsp grated ginger
2 green chillies, crushed
2 tsps vegetable oil
½ tsp black mustard seeds
A small sprig of curry leaves
¼ cup finely chopped fresh coriander
Salt to taste
Juice of 1 lime

For the dumplings, drain the lentils and pulse in a food processor with chillies, cumin seeds and very little water to make a thick smooth batter. The consistency should be of a cake batter.

Transfer to a bowl, add salt and mix. Cover and keep aside in a warm place to ferment for 4–5 hours. When fermented, mix in semolina.

Heat oil in a karahi or wok over medium heat. Add 1 tbsp of hot oil to the batter and whisk well.

Drop spoonfuls of batter into the hot oil and fry until the dumplings are golden, crisp and cooked through. Remove and drain on absorbent kitchen paper.

For the soup, cook the split pigeon peas with 1½ cups stock or water, turmeric and asafoetida in a pressure cooker. Wait for three whistles.

Whisk the cooked dal till smooth and transfer to a saucepan. Stir in the remaining stock or water, ginger and green chillies and bring to a boil.

In a small pan, heat oil over medium heat and temper the mustard seeds and curry leaves. When the mustard splutters, add this mixture to the lentil broth.

Add the fresh coriander and salt and simmer for 2 minutes. Remove from heat and mix in the lime juice.

Ladle the soup into bowls, top with the fried bondas and serve hot.

KALE CHANNE KI TARRI

My first taste of this black gram soup was on a harsh winter evening in Amritsar. After a quick visit to the Golden Temple, we went to visit my friend, Jyoti Arora, who made this wonderful soup for us. So delicious, filling and warming was the bowlful that I was quick to ask what went into it. And my friend shared this recipe without hesitance.

SERVES 4

- ¾ cup whole black gram (kala channa), soaked overnight in 2½ cups water
- 1½-inch piece of ginger, cut into juliennes
- 3 garlic cloves, finely sliced
- Salt to taste
- 4 cups vegetable stock or water
- 2 tsps butter
- 2 tsps all-purpose flour
- Freshly ground black pepper to taste

Transfer the channa along with the soaking water to a large saucepan. Add the ginger, garlic, salt and vegetable stock or water and bring to a boil over high heat. Stir occasionally, skimming off any scum that rises to the surface, till the gram is tender but not mushy. Strain and reserve the gram and broth separately.

Heat butter in a fresh pan over medium–low heat. When it melts, add flour and sauté until its raw flavour disappears. Whisk in the strained broth and bring to a boil.

When the broth thickens very slightly, add the channa and pepper.

Ladle into bowls and serve hot.

SOL KADHI

The tanginess of kokum has always fascinated me and I've never been tired of lending its unique sweet–sour flavour to as wide a variety of dishes as I can. The purplish hues of the dried fruit that most magically turns into a blushing pink when added to any liquid adds to the allure. Our long road journeys to Goa were incomplete without stopping at a Konkani eatery for lunch—a meal that started and ended with this soup!

SERVES 4

5–6 kokum petals
3 cups water
1 cup grated fresh coconut
1 tsp cumin seeds, lightly roasted
5 garlic cloves, finely chopped
2 green chillies, broken into pieces
Salt to taste
A few sprigs of fresh coriander

In a small saucepan, add kokum petals to a cup of water and bring to a boil over medium heat. Boil for 7–8 minutes until water turns deep red. Remove and cool slightly.

Pour the kokum water with the petals into a large blender, along with 1 ½ cups of water and the remaining ingredients except salt and fresh coriander. Blend into a smooth puree and strain into a bowl through cheesecloth. Squeeze out as much moisture as possible.

Transfer the strained solids to the blender again, add the rest of the water and blend again. Repeat the straining process. Discard solids.

Mix in salt and coriander. Refrigerate to chill.

Serve chilled.

BARANI SOUP

When I travel, I'm amazed at some of the cooking techniques in different communities and households. I witnessed cooking soup in jars in which pickles and grains are stored for the first time on a trip through Kerala. It's the baranis or jars that give the soup its name. The flavours of long-stored pickles come through in the dish until the last spoonful. Traditionally a slow-cooked soup, this version is much quicker but just as healthy and wholesome.

SERVES 4

- 3 litres mutton stock
- 3-inch cinnamon stick
- 3 cloves
- 3 green cardamom pods
- 1-inch piece of dry ginger or ¾ tsp ground dry ginger
- 200g mutton, cut into 2-inch pieces
- 2 tbsps ghee
- 1 tsp black mustard seeds
- 1 fresh curry leaf sprig, plus extra for garnish
- ¼ tsp fenugreek seeds, optional
- ¾ tsp crushed black peppercorns
- 2 large onions, finely sliced
- 2-inch piece of fresh ginger, cut into juliennes
- 2 tbsps raisins

In a large saucepan, add the stock, cinnamon, cloves, cardamom, dry ginger and mutton and bring to a boil over medium–high heat. Skim and discard any scum that rises to the surface.

Reduce the stock to half its volume (roughly 1½ litres), strain and keep aside. Reserve the mutton and stock, and discard the spices.

In a large heavy saucepan, heat ghee over medium heat and add mustard seeds, curry leaves, fenugreek seeds (if using) and peppercorns. Sauté them for a few seconds as they crackle until fragrant. Add onions and ginger and sauté until the onions turn light golden.

Add the raisins, sauté for a few seconds and stir in the strained stock. Reduce the heat to low and simmer, uncovered, till the stock reduces to 1 litre for about 8–10 minutes.

Add the mutton, simmer for a minute and remove from the heat.

Ladle into bowls and serve hot.

GOAN-STYLE CHICKEN AND CABBAGE SOUP

Goan cuisine is a strong confluence of Indo–Portuguese cooking. While many shun cabbage, it makes for a great addition to light soups as it adds body without heaviness. The beans not only add a soft bite but are also good plant protein. This soup is very light in flavour and perfect for those recovering from a bad cold or just want to keep things light. For a truly flavourful soup, make sure you use good stock.

SERVES 4

3 tbsps olive oil
4 garlic cloves, sliced
2 large spring onion stalks, sliced
4–6 cups vegetable stock
¾ cup cooked white beans
1 cup poached and shredded chicken
Salt to taste
1½ tsps freshly ground black pepper
¾ cup finely shredded green cabbage

In a large saucepan, heat olive oil, add garlic and spring onions and sauté until fragrant. Stir in the stock and simmer until the spring onions are tender.

Add the beans, chicken, salt and pepper. Cover the pan partially and simmer the soup for about 5 minutes.

Divide the shredded cabbage equally among four soup plates and ladle the simmering soup over it. Serve immediately.

ROASTED VEGETABLE AND FISH SOUP

When just starting out in college, I tried doing a tomato soup differently by charring the tomatoes and then pureeing them. The result was overwhelmingly delicious. Back then, the simple technique felt out of the box! I wasn't sure charred vegetables would go well with fish, but, when I tried it out, the combination worked surprisingly well. You could try this soup with only one variety of fish or a mixture of fish and shellfish to enjoy a different flavour with every bite.

SERVES 4

1 white fish fillet (250g)
6–7 cups vegetable or fish stock
6 large ripe tomatoes, halved lengthwise
1 large red bell pepper, quartered and deseeded
2 large onions, cut into wedges
4 large garlic cloves, peeled
2 tsps olive oil
2 tbsps chopped fresh basil
1 tsp paprika or red chilli powder
Salt to taste
Freshly ground black pepper to taste
A few fresh basil sprigs, for garnish

In a frying pan, place the fish fillet with 1–2 cups of stock and poach over low heat until fish is just cooked. Strain the stock and reserve. Cut the poached fish into small chunks.

Preheat the oven to 200°C.

Arrange tomatoes, cut side up, bell pepper, onions and garlic on a baking tray. Drizzle with olive oil, sprinkle the basil and spices and toss well. Roast the vegetables until brown and tender, turning over the pepper and onions occasionally—for about 25 minutes.

Remove the tray from the oven and allow the vegetables to cool. Then, transfer them, with the roasting juices, to a food processor or blender and puree until smooth.

Heat a saucepan, add the pureed vegetables and remaining stock and stir well. Allow the soup to come to a simmer.

Add the fish and simmer for 2–3 minutes.

Garnish with fresh basil and serve hot.

SALADS

Food can be at the centre of our moods, emotions and memories, and our understanding of it comes through our relationship with Earth. One of the most literal ways of celebrating this relationship is to enjoy ingredients in their natural form. And what better way is there to do this than a salad?

Growing up, salads were a mainstay at every meal at home. I, however, was always confused about 'green salad' at restaurants. When ordered, it would turn out to be a plateful of sliced onions, tomatoes and cucumber with a few lemon wedges. I could never find the green in it and had it not been for the sheer variety of salads I saw at home, I would've ended up thinking of salads as boring.

But nothing could be further from the truth.

A salad is a composition of flavours, textures and colours. From soft and smooth to crispy and crunchy, sweet and sour to spicy and creamy, there are no limits to what one can do with a salad. Even a simple mix of raw vegetables can be enhanced with dressings that can make one's heart sing. The main thing to remember in a salad, whether cold or warm, is that it should be absolutely fresh. Play with the amount of dressing to see what suits your palate best. Finally, don't be shy to tread into unfamiliar territory!

Hummus Salad

Home-Style Millet Salad

Assamese Pickled Tea Salad

Methi Microgreens Salad

Hara Channa Chaat

Mixed Greens with Greek Yoghurt

Bitter Gourd Crisps with Hung Curd Dip

Chicken Chaat

Green Tomato Roasted Garlic Salad with Peppered Lamb

Pan-Grilled Prawn Salad

HUMMUS SALAD

Hummus is a global dish I'm partial to. It was my comfort food when I was in Kuwait and I enjoyed eating it with kuboos and a basil salad. I always thought of it as sunset on a plate, thanks to the bright cherry tomatoes and dashes of paprika that reminded me of a blushing sky—not to mention that my mealtime was at sunset.

SERVES 4

Hummus

2 cups boiled chickpeas (skin removed)
3 tbsps tahini or sesame paste
3–4 garlic cloves
1 tsp cumin seeds, lightly roasted
2 tbsps lemon juice
¼ cup olive oil
1 tsp paprika

Salad

1 cup mixed cherry tomatoes, halved
¼ cup roughly chopped basil leaves
¼ cup pitted olives (any variety)
¼ cup olive oil
Salt to taste
Freshly ground black pepper to taste

Wash and rinse the boiled and cleaned chickpeas. Transfer to a blender or food processor, add tahini, garlic and cumin, and blend until the mixture is smooth and creamy.

Transfer the hummus to a mixing bowl and add the lemon juice. Drizzle evenly with olive oil and sprinkle paprika.

For the salad, in a clean bowl, lightly crush the cherry tomatoes with a fork. Add basil, olives, olive oil, salt and pepper. Toss quickly.

Serve dollops of hummus into four plates, pile some salad over each dollop and serve.

TIP

The hummus can also be served chilled.

HOME-STYLE MILLET SALAD

Sometimes, a simple meal is the best meal. My friend Angeline taught me how to make this salad when I was on a strict diet. The recipe quickly became a favourite because it's simple, light, wholesome, fresh and immensely delightful to eat. The healthy quotient is easily masked by the rainbow of colours and textures!

SERVES 2–3

1 cup mixed millets
3 cups water
½ cup onions, finely chopped
½ cup tomatoes, finely chopped
¼ cup fresh coriander, finely chopped
1 large red bell pepper, diced or julienned
1 green zucchini, diced

Dressing

1 tbsp coconut oil
Juice of 1 lemon
½ tsp paprika
¼ cup pumpkin seeds, toasted
¼ tsp salt
½ tsp black pepper

In a pan, add the millets and water and bring to a boil over medium–low heat. Cover partially and cook, stirring occasionally until the millets are tender.

Drain the liquid and rinse the millets under cold water. Drain all the moisture and transfer into a mixing bowl. Set aside to cool. Add the vegetables and toss well together.

For the dressing, whisk all the ingredients together in a small mixing bowl.

Drizzle over the salad, toss quickly and serve.

ASSAMESE PICKLED TEA SALAD

Panic can be inspiring sometimes and this salad is a case in point! It was born during a food-and-tea–pairing workshop when the supplier failed to turn up with half of the ingredients that had been requested. The original pesto was a smashing hit but the one thing I've changed here is that I've given the salad a day's resting time to help the flavours meld together.

SERVES 4

Tea pesto

½ cup Sencha green tea leaves (or any other mild green tea leaves)
2 cups hot water
3–4 garlic cloves
½-inch piece of ginger (optional)
2 tsps white natural vinegar
2 tbsps sesame oil
¼ cup walnuts

Salad

2 cups mixed salad leaves
1 small fennel bulb, shaved into fine slices
1 large onion, sliced into fine rings
¼ cup sunflower seeds
1 tbsp toasted sesame seeds
4 garlic cloves, sliced and fried crisp, for garnish

Place the tea leaves in a clean mixing bowl and pour hot water over them. Cover and set aside for 10–15 minutes.

Drain the water, rinse the tea leaves and immerse in cold water. Cover and set aside for an hour, then drain again and gently squeeze the tea leaves to drain excess water.

Transfer to a blender, add the rest of the ingredients and blend into a coarse pesto. Transfer into a jar and set aside in a cool dry place overnight.

To compile salad, place a dollop of tea pesto in the centre of four serving plates or soup plates and arrange salad ingredients around it, or just mix it all together. Garnish with fried garlic and serve.

METHI MICROGREENS SALAD

Microgreens are the new superfood, and growing them on the balcony or verandah is easy. I love using them in rotis and parathas and as toppings on a variety of dishes. Microgreens are more than just a garnish. They can be used in salads and mains, lending a whole new dimension to food as we know it.

SERVES 2–3

2 tsps olive oil
2 tsps apple cider vinegar
1 tsp garlic paste
¼ tsp dried herbs
Salt to taste
Black pepper powder to taste
¼ tsp red chilli powder
1 large tomato, diced
2 cups fenugreek microgreens, washed, drained and pat-dried

Put all the ingredients except tomato and microgreens in a small jar with a tight-fitting lid. Close the jar and shake it well, until the oil and vinegar turn frothy.

Combine tomato and microgreens in a mixing bowl and pour the dressing over them. Toss quickly and portion into serving plates.

Serve immediately.

HARA CHANNA CHAAT

There was a time not too long ago when a stroll on one of the many beaches of Mumbai was considered a waste if one had not invested in a paper cone of this spicy tangy chaat. It set the mouth on fire, yet it was so addictive that you couldn't stop having more. Today, this is a rare treat on a beach, but thankfully can be easily made at home. The best thing about it is that green chickpeas are seasonal and can be easily substituted with black chickpeas or even garbanzo beans soaked overnight, giving you a new chaat each time.

SERVES 2–3

4 cups water
1 heaped tbsp salt, plus more to taste
¼ tsp turmeric powder (optional)
¼ tsp asafoetida
¼ tsp cumin seeds
2 cups fresh green chickpeas, cleaned, washed and rinsed
2 tbsps oil
Juice of 2 limes
1 large onion, finely chopped
1 large tomato, finely chopped
2 tbsps fresh coriander, finely chopped
½ tsp dried mango powder
½ tsp fennel powder
1 tsp red chilli powder
½ tsp coriander powder

In a saucepan, add water, salt, turmeric, asafoetida and cumin seeds and bring to a rolling boil over high heat. Add chickpeas, reduce heat to medium and cook for 5–7 minutes until the chickpeas are tender but firm to bite. (They can also be steamed.)

Drain the chickpeas and transfer to a large mixing bowl. Allow to cool to room temperature.

Add remaining ingredients and toss well. Serve immediately.

MIXED GREENS WITH GREEK YOGHURT

Yoghurt, with its great probiotic qualities, is a favourite across India in its many avatars, from raita to shrikhand, lassi and kadhi. This recipe is inspired by a whole mung raita I was treated to in a village during an unusually hot summer. The simple dish was not only cooling but also filling and very flavourful. I've substituted plain yoghurt with Greek yoghurt and upped the nutrition quota by using sprouted mung instead of whole.

SERVES 4

- 1 medium onion, sliced into wedges
- 2 tbsps apple cider vinegar
- ½ tsp mixed dried herbs
- 1 cup Greek yoghurt
- 1 cup sprouted green mung and channa in equal proportions
- 1 English cucumber, unpeeled and diced
- Salt to taste
- Freshly ground black pepper to taste
- 200g mixed baby salad leaves (spinach, red spinach, kale, mixed lettuce)
- ¼ cup alfalfa sprouts
- ¼ cup almond halves, roasted
- 2 tbsps extra-virgin olive oil
- 1 tsp apple cider vinegar from the pickling onion
- 1 garlic clove, crushed
- ½ tsp red chilli flakes

Place the onion in a small mixing bowl or mason jar and add vinegar and herbs. Mix well (or tighten the jar top and give it a good shake). Set aside for 15–20 minutes.

Meanwhile, whisk the Greek yoghurt until smooth. Add the sprouts, cucumber, salt and pepper. Mix well, cover and refrigerate.

Cut away any thick stems from the salad leaves using a paring knife, and place the leaves in a mixing bowl. Remove the onion from the vinegar and add to the salad along with the alfalfa sprouts.

To make the dressing, whisk together oil, vinegar, garlic, salt and pepper in a small bowl. Set aside for 10 minutes.

Pour the dressing over the salad leaves and toss well. Divide equally among four salad plates. Place a dollop of Greek yoghurt sprout mix on one side, sprinkle over with almond halves and serve.

BITTER GOURD CRISPS WITH HUNG CURD DIP

The karela or bitter gourd is known to be the best vegetable for controlling blood sugar. I spent many years strongly disliking the vegetable until I came across these crisps. Bitter with the right hint of salt and pepper, these make for a wonderful salad as well as a tea-time snack.

SERVES 4

Crisps

- 250g bitter gourd, halved lengthwise, seeds and pith removed
- 1 ¼ cup brine (2 tbsps salt dissolved in 1 ¼ cups water)
- 2 tbsps olive oil
- 1 medium onion, finely sliced
- ½ tsp salt
- ½ tsp black pepper powder

Dip

- ½ cup hung curd
- ¼ tsp freshly ground black pepper
- ¼ tsp sea salt
- 1 heaped tsp freshly chopped tulsi/dill/coriander

Cut the bitter gourd into juliennes. Transfer to a mixing bowl. Pour the brine over it, stir once and set aside for an hour.

Drain the brine and rinse the bitter gourd in cold water. Pat dry using a kitchen towel.

Heat olive oil in a frying pan over medium–high heat, add onions and sauté until golden. Remove and drain on absorbent paper.

Add the gourd to the same pan and fry until golden and crisp. Remove, drain the excess oil on absorbent paper and transfer to a mixing bowl. Immediately toss with salt and pepper.

Add the fried onions and toss well.

For the dip, mix the ingredients together. Serve dollops with the crisps.

CHICKEN CHAAT SALAD

Gorging on chaat and its many variations is a great Indian pastime. Contrary to the popular belief, chaats are not limited to chickpeas, papdi and fritters, but also include a range of chicken and mutton delicacies. It was a talented chef working in a famous club who first thought of adding a healthy aspect to chaats. This salad is a take on a chicken chaat I sampled in Chhattisgarh and tastes equally good even without chicken.

SERVES 4–5

- 1 tbsp vegetable oil
- 1 medium green chilli, finely chopped (optional)
- 2 large garlic cloves, finely chopped
- 1 onion, finely chopped
- ¼ cup tomato puree
- 1 tbsp garam masala
- 2 × 150g chicken breasts, diced
- Salt to taste
- 1 large cucumber, diced
- 1 cup cherry tomatoes, halved
- 2 tsps chaat masala
- ½ cup arugula leaves
- ½ cup peanuts, roasted
- ½ cup fresh coriander, finely chopped
- Juice of 2 limes

Heat oil in a large frying pan over low heat, add chilli, garlic and onion and sauté until the onion turns golden.

Add tomato puree, garam masala and chicken and cook until the chicken is tender, and the sauce coats the chicken thickly.

Add salt, mix well and cook for a few seconds. Remove pan from the heat and transfer the chicken to a bowl.

Add the remaining ingredients, mix well and serve immediately.

GREEN TOMATO ROASTED GARLIC SALAD WITH PEPPERED LAMB

I encountered the freshest green tomatoes in Bandhavgarh, Madhya Pradesh, on a farm. Instantly inspired, I'd made a simpler version of this salad, but later added more elements to make it wholesome. The sourness of green tomatoes and sweetish tang of pickled beets pair wonderfully with the spicy roast lamb, making this a perfect warm salad for winter evenings.

SERVES 4–6

Lamb

1 tbsp olive oil
5 dry red Kashmiri chillies, broken into pieces
1 tsp crushed black pepper
½ tsp salt
200g boneless lamb

Salad

5–6 fresh large green tomatoes, cut into wedges
2 tbsps extra-virgin olive oil
Salt to taste
Freshly ground black pepper to taste
10 small garlic cloves
2 soft boiled eggs, peeled and halved
8–10 pickled onion rings and carrot slices each (see note)
1 small iceberg lettuce head, cored and cut

Preheat the oven to 150°C.

Add olive oil, Kashmiri chillies, crushed pepper and salt in a pan and mix well. Heat the pan on low heat until the oil is hot but not smoking. Remove from the heat and allow the oil to cool. Transfer the chilli pepper oil to a mixing bowl.

Slice the lamb finely and toss it with the chillies. Spread evenly on a baking tray, cover with foil and bake for 40 minutes or until done. Cool and shred the meat.

On a separate baking tray, toss the green tomato wedges with olive oil, salt, pepper and garlic. Roast for 5–7 minutes in the oven until the tomatoes soften slightly.

Toss the shredded lamb with tomatoes, soft-boiled eggs and pickled onions and carrots. Line serving plates with lettuce and arrange the salad in them. Serve immediately.

NOTE: To make the pickled onion rings and carrots, cut a large onion into fine rings and peel and slice a large carrot. Mix together a cup of vinegar with 1 tbsp dried herbs, two bay leaves, 3–4 cloves, 1 tsp salt and 1 tsp red chilli flakes in a pan. Add onion rings and carrot slices and bring to a boil. Reduce heat so the mixture can simmer for 5–8 minutes. When done, transfer to a clean dry jar and allow to cool completely before closing the lid. Allow to mature for 3–4 days before refrigerating. This pickle can also be used in sandwiches.

PAN-GRILLED PRAWN SALAD

Millets, the new superfood, have been consumed in India since time immemorial and are a unique substitute for all things gluten. Many types of millets are dying out as farmers are not growing them due to lack of demand, owing to our limited knowledge of their versatility. This salad is a good example of the ways in which millets can be used. Here, they have been paired with succulent prawns to make a quick mini meal.

SERVES 4

Prawns

1 tsp olive oil
Freshly squeezed juice of 2 oranges or 1 lemon
¼ tsp salt
¼ tsp crushed pepper
1 cup fresh prawns, shelled and deveined

Millets

1 cup vegetable stock, or more as required
1–2 large garlic cloves
2 fresh oregano sprigs or ¼ tsp dried oregano
½ cup finger millets or barley
1 small zucchini, finely diced
4–5 button mushrooms, sliced
Juice of 1 lime
1 large onion, finely diced
½ cup mixed salad leaves or baby spinach leaves

In a mixing bowl, whisk together olive oil, orange or lemon juice, salt and pepper. Add prawns, toss well and set aside for 10 minutes.

Meanwhile, prepare the millets. Add vegetable stock, garlic and oregano to a large frying pan and bring to a simmer.

Add millets, cover and cook until the millets are tender and the moisture has dried up. If the millets are undercooked, add more stock in ¼ cups and cook.

Add the zucchini and mushrooms to the hot mixture and leave to cool.

When done, fluff the millets with a fork, mix well with the salad leaves and set aside.

Place a griddle or grill pan on medium–high heat and grill the marinated prawns for a minute on each side, brushing with the marinade to keep them from drying out.

Top the millet salad with the cooked prawns and serve immediately.

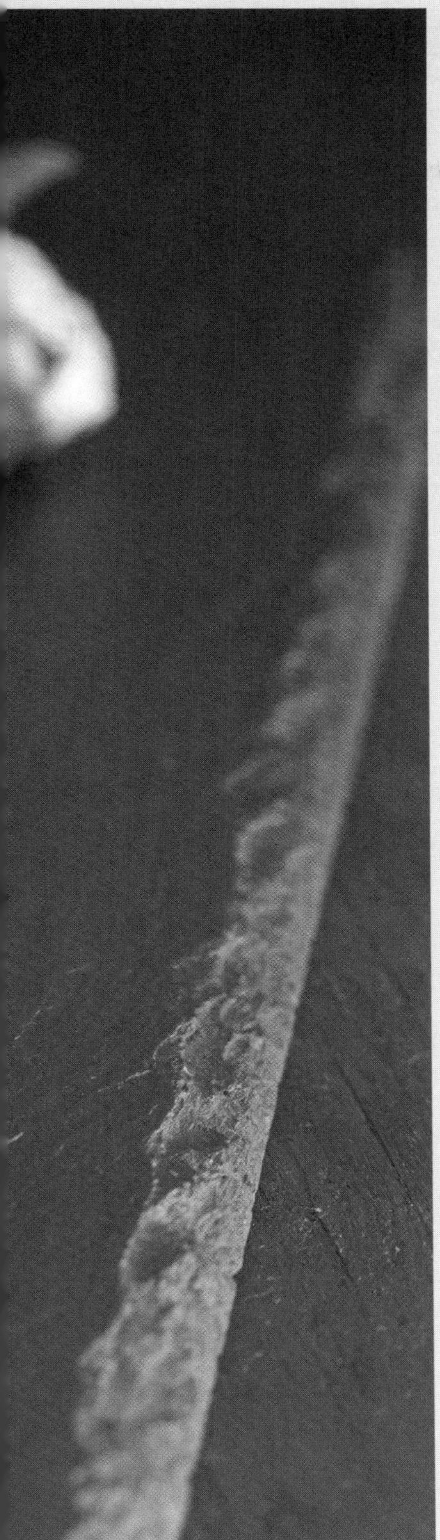

STARTERS

In India, we love to eat at any time, be it between meals when we are at home or when we are travelling and have nothing better to do than look out of the window and watch the world go by. Travelling in India can, at times, be hard for those on any kind of diet, because, at every turn, station or highway, one is tempted by enticing aromas of snacks. Kachori, samosa, chaat, bhel puri, pani puri, wada pav and bhajiya—you name it and you've got it. It's the same at any party or outing with family where we order starters that are usually deep-fried and heavy on spice and salt. A healthy diet goes for a toss and, having succumbed to temptation, one spends a good hour or two talking oneself out of guilt.

For the home too, choices of health-based snacks are limited, and the ready-to-eat or cooked stuff available in supermarkets are barely healthy. You end up feeling that being on a diet is akin to punishment. That need not be the case.

There are many snacks and starters one can easily make at home with a bit of planning. Once you get used to home-made goodies, you won't crave oily, salty snacks. Treat these recipes as templates and experiment with as many ingredients as you want. You'll be surprised to see how many options open up!

Golden Black Rice Arancini

Drumstick Garlic Roast

Quinoa and Mixed Bean Patties

Holy Basil Mushroom

Pepper-Crusted Yam

Tofu Shashlik

Bitter Gourds Stuffed with Prawns

Barbequed Spicy Chicken Legs

Assamese-Style Smoked Pork

Pink Pepper and Chilli Glaze Lamb Chops

GOLDEN BLACK RICE ARANCINI

I had arancini when I was travelling in Milan. It was a cold day and the smoking hot dish was the ultimate comfort food—fried, creamy, filled with cheese—and unfortunately one that sent me on a guilt trip. Black rice from Mizoram makes an excellent substitute for Arborio. Here, I've tried to tackle the guilt by baking the rice instead of deep-frying.

SERVES 4–6

2 tsps olive oil
½ tsp minced black garlic (see page 28)
¼ cup red onions, finely chopped
1 cup black rice, washed, soaked for 40 minutes and drained
¼ cup mushrooms, finely chopped
4 cups vegetable stock, plus more if required
¼ cup grated vegan cheese
2 tbsps olives, finely chopped
Salt to taste
2 cups panko crumbs mixed with 2 tbsps olive oil

Chia pesto

3 tbsps chia seeds, soaked in ½ cup water for 30 minutes
1 cup fresh basil leaves
¼ cup chopped walnuts
2 tbsps chopped garlic or garlic chives
1 tsp sea salt
1 tsp lemon juice
¼ cup olive oil

In a saucepan, heat olive oil over medium heat, add garlic and onions and cook until the onions are translucent. Add the black rice and mushrooms and sauté for a minute. Pour the stock and cook, stirring occasionally, until the rice is slightly overcooked, for about 30–45 minutes. Add more stock if required.

When done, transfer the rice to a clean bowl and mix in cheese, olives and salt.

Preheat the oven to 180°C. Line a baking tray with parchment paper.

When the rice has cooled, divide into lime-sized portions and roll into arancini (balls). Coat them evenly with panko crumbs by rolling the balls in the panko mixture, arrange on the baking tray and refrigerate for 10 minutes.

Meanwhile, blend all the pesto ingredients into a smooth paste. Transfer to a bowl or jar and refrigerate.

Remove the arancini from the fridge and bake for 15–20 minutes until crisp and slightly coloured.

Serve hot with chia pesto.

DRUMSTICK GARLIC ROAST

My trips to Manipal, a small university town in coastal Karnataka, are often special as I not only enjoy interacting with budding chefs at the country's premier hospitality school, but also because that's where I get to taste some of the best and most unique foods in India. This drumstick garlic roast is one such dish, unique and highly recommended by students—a recommendation I am forever grateful for!

SERVES 4

1 tbsp coriander seeds
1 tsp fenugreek seeds
1 heaped tsp cumin seeds
5 dry red chillies, stems and seeds removed
1 tsp black peppercorns
1 large sprig of curry leaves
5 garlic cloves
3 large drumsticks
3 cups water
1 tsp salt, plus to taste
2 tbsps tamarind paste
1 tbsp coconut oil

Roast coriander, fenugreek and cumin seeds in a pan over medium–low heat until fragrant. Add chillies, peppercorns, curry leaves and garlic, and continue to roast until the garlic is golden.

Cool the mixture, then grind to a fine powder in a spice grinder.

String or peel the drumsticks with a small knife to remove any thick fibrous skin. Cut them into finger-length pieces.

Bring water and salt to a boil and add the drumsticks. Turn off the heat and allow the drumsticks to soak for 5–7 minutes.

Drain the water and make lengthwise slits in the drumsticks. Transfer to a mixing bowl, add a tablespoon of the spice mix and tamarind paste and toss well. Set aside for 10 minutes.

Heat coconut oil in a karahi on low heat. Add the marinated drumsticks and toss well, adding salt if required. Cook for 2–3 minutes on high heat until the drumsticks are slightly tender and very slightly charred. Serve hot.

QUINOA AND MIXED BEAN PATTIES

Patties, cutlets and tikkis are a favourite among most people. The crisp exterior and soft insides are addictive. But people tend to refrain from them because the main ingredient is potatoes. That doesn't always have to be the case. Here, the patties are filled with quinoa, lentils and sprouts—sure to please any palate without raising fear of elevating sugar levels.

SERVES 4–8

1 cup quinoa
1 cup lentils
4 cups vegetable stock
1 cup mixed bean sprouts
½ cup barley, cooked
Salt to taste
Freshly ground black pepper to taste
1 tsp ginger–garlic paste
½ tsp chaat masala
2 tbsps lemon juice
½ cup arrowroot flour
½ cup coriander leaves, freshly chopped
2 tbsps of oil for shallow-frying

In a saucepan, lightly toast the quinoa and lentils on medium–low heat. Add the stock and bean sprouts and bring to a boil. Cook until the quinoa and lentils are cooked through and sprouts are tender.

Add the remaining ingredients and gently mash everything together.

Divide the mixture into small lime-sized balls and flatten each ball into a patty.

Brush a frying pan with oil and place on low heat. Arrange the patties on the pan and gently fry on both sides until golden brown.

Serve hot with a nice chutney or sauce. (The chia pesto on page 78 and chilli jam on page 97 will make equally delicious accompaniments.)

HOLY BASIL MUSHROOMS

I was quite amused when I first heard one of my Le Cordon Bleu teachers say that green chutney is India's answer to Italy's pesto. 'The reverse could be equally true,' I thought to myself, as I fought back the desire to proclaim that chutney probably came first. But I kept quiet as the chef drew parallels to prove the versatility of the green chutney. It can be used as a dip, an accompaniment, a marinade, curry base and even added to mayonnaise for sandwich fillings. Here, I've given my own twist to this Indian must-have by substituting mint with holy basil. I love the result—I hope you do too!

SERVES 4–6

- 1½ cups freshly chopped coriander
- ½ cup holy basil (tulsi) leaves
- 3 green chillies, deseeded and chopped
- 8 garlic cloves, chopped
- 1 tsp cumin seeds
- 1 tsp poppy seeds
- 1 tbsp coriander seeds
- 6 black peppercorns
- 1 tsp sesame seeds
- 1 tsp turmeric powder
- 3 tbsps water
- 3 cups quartered button mushrooms (large)
- A pinch of salt
- A pinch of crushed black pepper
- 2 tbsps olive oil
- A few fresh parsley sprigs, for garnish

Toss the coriander, basil, chillies and garlic in a bowl together and set aside.

Dry-roast each spice (except turmeric) separately in a pan on low heat until fragrant. Transfer to a blender along with turmeric and the coriander–basil mix and blend to a smooth thick paste, adding water as required.

Transfer the paste to a clean mixing bowl and add the remaining ingredients. Toss well to coat the mushrooms evenly. Set aside for 10 minutes.

Preheat the oven to 175°C.

Place the marinated mushrooms on a lightly greased baking tray and bake for 10–15 minutes. Alternately, you can toss the mushrooms in a hot pan for 5 minutes.

Garnish with fresh parsley and serve hot.

PEPPER-CRUSTED YAM

The variety of yam available across India is amazing and I first encountered purple yam on a trip to Andhra Pradesh. As far as superfoods go, it's great for diabetics. Here, pink pepper adds a distinct flavour to this earthy vegetable.

SERVES 4

400g purple yam, cut into thick batons
½ tsp garam masala powder
1 large onion, minced
3–4 garlic cloves, minced
Salt to taste
4–5 cups vegetable stock or water
1 tbsp tamarind paste
2 tsps peppercorns
1 tsp fennel seeds
½ tsp cumin seeds
½ cup semolina
Oil for shallow-frying

In a pan, add yam, garam masala, onion, garlic, salt and stock or water and boil on high heat. Cook until the yam is cooked yet firm enough to hold shape. Alternately, steam the yam.

When done, drain the yam properly. Transfer to a mixing bowl, add tamarind paste and toss carefully. Set aside.

Grind peppercorns, fennel and cumin seeds together in a spice grinder into a coarse powder.

In a bowl, mix the spice powder with semolina and salt and spread it out on a small plate.

Roll the batons in the spiced semolina mixture and shallow-fry on a griddle on medium heat until they turn golden and slightly crispy on the surface.

Serve hot with any salad of your choice.

TOFU SHASHLIK

I always liked tofu, but I really fell in love with it when I went to Hong Kong and visited a shop that only sold tofu. It was an eye-opening, palate-teasing experience—shelf upon shelf was laden with tofu of different textures, flavours and colours. The shopkeeper was kind enough to offer me a taste of a wide variety, explaining the nuances between each. Since then, I've experimented with various types but, in the end, I always return to the comfort of plain tofu because it allows me to play with an endless array of flavours.

SERVES 4

- 6–8 large garlic cloves
- 6–8 black peppercorns
- ½ tsp coriander powder
- ½ tsp cumin powder
- Salt to taste
- 2–3 tbsps olive oil
- Juice and rind of 1 large orange
- ¼ cup vegetable stock
- 500g plain tofu, cut into cubes
- 1 red, green and yellow capsicum each, cut into large dices
- ½ cup large button mushrooms
- ¼ cup mixed olives, deseeded
- 8 bamboo skewers, soaked in water

Dry-roast garlic and peppercorns in a small frying pan on low heat until the garlic turns golden and the pepper is smoky. Transfer to a blender, add the spices, salt, oil, juice and rind of the orange and stock and blend well.

Transfer marinade to a large mixing bowl, add tofu, capsicum, mushrooms and olives and toss well to coat evenly. Cover and set aside for half an hour.

Pat dry the skewers and mount the tofu and vegetables onto them, alternating the colours and textures.

Heat a grill pan or griddle on high heat and place the skewers over it. Rotate the shashliks every few seconds and brush with marinade until they are slightly charred all over.

Serve immediately with a salad of your choice.

BITTER GOURDS STUFFED WITH PRAWNS

This is a traditional dish belonging to the East Indian community, the original inhabitants of Mumbai. When the Portuguese from the East India Company married the locals, a new cuisine was born, combining Indian ingredients with Portuguese flavours and techniques. This dish is one such example, with a few tiny twists. Remember to use small, young and tender gourds for best results.

SERVES 4

8 baby bitter gourds, washed well and pat-dried
1 ½ cups water mixed with 3 tsps salt

Filling

2 tbsps clarified butter or olive oil
1 onion, finely chopped
4 garlic cloves, finely chopped
2 green chillies, finely chopped
1 ½ cups prawns, shelled and deveined
1 tomato, finely chopped
½ tsp garam masala powder
½ tsp fennel powder
Salt to taste
1 tsp black pepper powder
2 tsps fresh parsley, finely chopped
Cotton strings, soaked in water
Oil for shallow-frying
1 tsp chaat masala, for garnish

Slice off both ends of the bitter gourds and slit them lengthwise, taking care not to cut them into half. Carefully scoop out the seeds and flesh with a spoon. Place in salted water and set aside for an hour.

Meanwhile, for the filling, heat clarified butter or olive oil in a pan on medium heat. Add onion and garlic and sauté until the onion turns golden. Add the remaining ingredients and cook, stirring occasionally until the prawns are cooked through. Turn off the heat and remove pan.

Drain the water from the gourds. With a small spoon, stuff the filling into the slits, then tie up each gourd using the soaked cotton strings to seal the filling.

Place a pan on low heat and drizzle liberally with oil. Shallow-fry the stuffed gourds, turning at regular intervals until they're tender.

When done, arrange on serving plates and cut the strings. Sprinkle with chaat masala and serve.

BARBEQUED SPICY CHICKEN LEGS

On my first trip to Amritsar, a friend and I decided to sample the local tandoori chicken. We overconfidently ordered two plates and decided to face the challenge when two whole spicy roasted chickens were placed in front of us. I was so stuffed, I returned to the hotel crawling on my knees but with the satisfaction of not only polishing off one whole chicken by myself, but also of spying on the man who made the marinade and noting the recipe!

SERVES 4

8 chicken drumsticks
3 cups water mixed with 2 tsps salt
½ cup buttermilk
1 tbsp red chilli powder
1 tsp cumin–coriander powder in equal proportions
½ tsp black pepper powder
½ tsp fenugreek seeds, roasted and powdered
½ tsp turmeric powder
1 tbsp garlic paste
Salt to taste
2 tbsps vegetable oil
2 tbsps butter, melted
Lemon wedges to serve

Soak the drumsticks in the salted water for 20 minutes.

Meanwhile, in a large bowl, mix together buttermilk, spices, garlic paste and salt and whisk well.

Drain the water, rinse the chicken and add to the bowl of spiced buttermilk. Toss well, cover and set aside for 30 minutes.

Preheat the oven to 220°C. Arrange the marinated chicken on a baking tray lined with foil and roast for 4–6 minutes until half-done.

Whisk vegetable oil and butter together and brush over the chicken. Turn the pieces over, cover with foil and roast for another 4–5 minutes until tender.

Remove from the oven and serve hot with lemon wedges.

ASSAMESE-STYLE SMOKED PORK

A dish from north-east India, smoked meat was a favourite of English sahibs and army personnel stationed in the region. Sun-dried meat is a local favourite. I first tasted sun-dried meat, thanks to Nick, an Assamese student I met during a workshop at a college. It was a bit of an acquired taste but I soon got hooked to it. Though traditionally sun-dried, here I've oven-roasted the meat, then smoked it to make this dish easier to prepare for home-cooks.

SERVES 4–6

2 tbsps mustard oil
1 tbsp stuffed red chilli pickle
2 onions, roughly chopped
Salt to taste
500g pork tenderloin, cut into thin strips
3 large onions, sliced

For smoking

4–5 coals
1 large dried red chilli
2 tsps oil

Blend mustard oil, chilli pickle, roughly chopped onions and salt into a smooth paste. Transfer to a large mixing bowl.

Add the tenderloin strips and lightly rub the marinade on them. Cover and set aside for 30 minutes.

Heat a pan and sauté the onion slices until golden, but not dark brown. Arrange the tenderloin strips on the bed of sliced onions and slow-cook for 10 minutes.

Turn the pieces over and brush with any marinade remaining in the bowl, cover and roast for another 10 minutes.

When done, transfer the meat to a large plate. Clear some space in the centre.

Heat the coals on a flame until red-hot. Using a pair of tongs, carefully place them at the centre of the plate and place a red chilli over them.

Drizzle oil over the coals and as soon as they begin to smoke, cover the plate with a large bowl turned upside. Allow the meat to smoke for 5–6 minutes or until the smoke settles.

Serve immediately with a salad of your choice.

PINK PEPPER AND CHILLI GLAZE LAMB CHOPS

Pink pepper is more a berry than a pepper, but its flavour packs the same punch. Chilli jam would seem a surprising inclusion in a book for those who refrain from sugar, but this recipe is perfect for cheat days when you want to sneak in a bit of sweetness to balance out other flavours. Together, this sweet-and-spicy combination paired with the citrusy freshness of orange will work wonders when you want to entertain guests or are in the mood to celebrate.

SERVES 4

- 1 cup red wine
- ¾ tsp black salt
- 1 tsp crushed pink peppercorns
- 2 tsps finely chopped garlic
- 1 tsp finely chopped ginger
- 1 tbsp chilli jam (see note)
- 1 tsp smoked sweet paprika
- 1 tbsp grated orange rind
- 8 lamb chops
- 3 tbsps olive oil

In a large bowl, whisk together all the ingredients except lamb chops and oil. Mix well, cover and set aside for 20 minutes to allow the flavours to merge.

Add the lamb chops and toss well. Marinate for 20–30 minutes. Meanwhile, preheat the oven to 180°C.

Heat a grill pan on high heat until it's hot. Drizzle with olive oil, and pan-sear the lamb chops for 3 minutes on each side. Transfer to a lightly greased baking tray and bake in the oven for 10–15 minutes or till done, occasionally basting with the marinade.

When done, rest the meat for a few minutes before serving.

Serve with a nice crisp salad on the side.

NOTE: Chilli jam is easily available in supermarkets everywhere but if you want to avoid the sugar you can make an easier glaze at home. Mix together half a cup of freshly squeezed orange juice with a tablespoon of jaggery and a teaspoon of red chilli flakes. Cook on low heat until it's glossy. Cool and use.

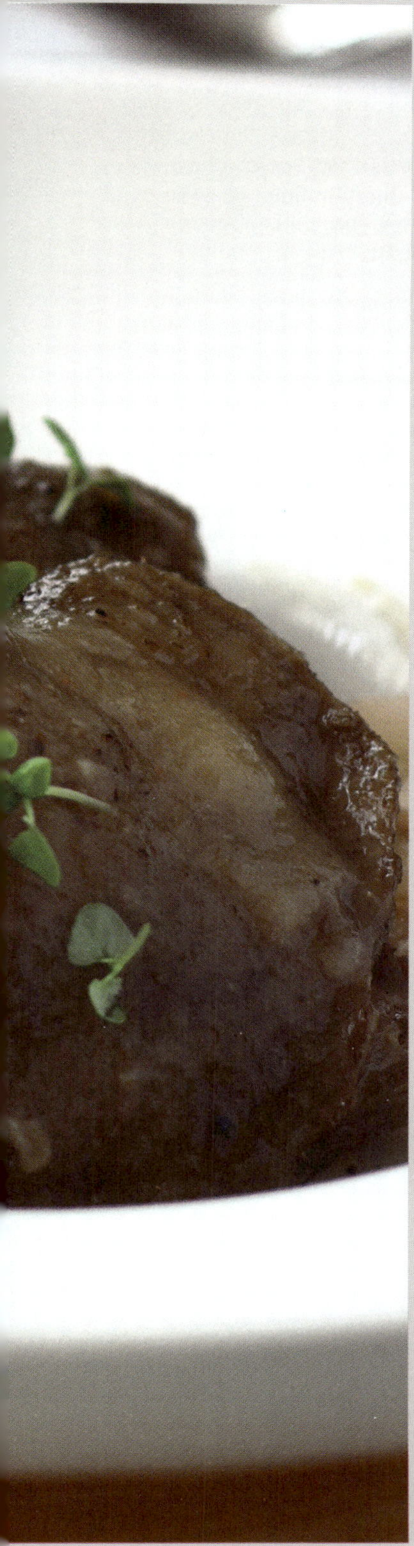

MAINS

Food is about so much more than just recipes; it's about the geography, history and evolution of ingredients, cooking techniques and taking the positives aspects of our past and applying them to our future. A big step we can take towards our own healing and well-being is observing what changes occur in our bodies during each season. It's also about taking advantage of the fresh foodstuffs nature offers each season and trusting her wisdom when cooking.

Simple meals do not have to be boring. They can be nutritious and flavourful at the same time! The use of proper cooking techniques and applying them to new combinations of fresh produce, flavouring and spices not only enhance food but also make the journey towards healing a tastier one.

One's diet may change with the onset of diabetes, but a proper, healthy diet also helps control or reverse it. The adage of eat responsibly comes to mind. Consuming foods that are local and seasonal are a big help and good for a sustainable way of life.

ALLOO PAATAL BHAJI

Literally meaning 'thin curry', this simple and traditional recipe features on weekly menus across homes in Maharashtra. Alloo here is not the misspelt Hindi word for potato, but the Marathi word for colocasia. Colocasia is a rich source of minerals, and this recipe, complete with peanuts, coconut and chickpea flour, also has a fair share of protein and good fat. Tamarind not only adds a delicious tang to the curry but also combats an itchy throat sometimes brought on by colocasia.

SERVES 3–4

- 8–10 colocasia leaves, washed and wiped dry
- 2 tbsps raw peanuts
- ¼ cup coconut slivers
- 2 tbsps chickpea flour (besan)
- 1 tsp cumin seeds
- 1 tsp red chilli powder
- ½ tsp turmeric powder
- ¼ tsp asafoetida, plus a pinch
- 3 cups vegetable stock or water
- ¼ cup tamarind pulp
- Salt to taste
- 2 tsps oil
- ¼ tsp mustard seeds
- 1 tsp garlic slices

Using the tip of a small sharp knife, remove the thick veins from each leaf.

Finely chop the cleaned leaves and add to a strainer with peanuts. Place the strainer over a pot of boiling water and steam for 10 minutes. When done, mash the steamed leaves lightly.

Heat a heavy pan over medium heat, add the coconut slivers and roast gently until golden and fragrant. Add the mashed leaves, flour, spices and asafoetida and mix well.

Gradually stir in vegetable stock or water, taking care to avoid the flour getting lumpy. Mix well and cook on low heat, stirring until the curry is the consistency of a creamy soup. Stir in the tamarind pulp. Simmer for 5 minutes.

Meanwhile, heat oil in a small pan and temper the pinch of asafoetida, mustard and garlic. When the garlic turns crisp, immediately pour the tempering over the curry after the heat is turned off and cover with a tight lid.

Allow flavours to merge for 4–5 minutes. Serve hot with wheat or millet rotis.

TIP

In case tamarind is unavailable, 3 cups of water or stock can be easily substituted with 1 cup of yoghurt whisked with 2 cups of water. This will lend the curry the desired tang.

VALAIPOO MURUNGAI KEERAI VARUVAL

My favourite morning sight is drumsticks hanging from a tree with gentle rays of the sun passing through the leaves. There was a tree in my neighbourhood and, as kids, we would take a long stick with a tiny hook attached to it and pull off the drumsticks. Such fun! Today, drumsticks and its leaves are popular as a superfood. Here, the leaves have been paired with yet another delicious, healthy ingredient—banana blossoms.

SERVES 4

- 2 tsps sesame oil
- 1 tsp mustard seeds
- 1 tbsp split Bengal gram (chana dal)
- 2 large fresh red chillies or dried red chillies, broken into bits
- 5–6 shallots, minced
- ¼ tsp ground turmeric (optional)
- 1 large banana blossom, cleaned (see note)
- 1 cup drumstick leaves
- Salt to taste
- ¼ cup grated fresh coconut, for garnish

Heat oil in a large frying pan on medium heat and add mustard seeds, split gram and chillies. When the mustard is crackling, add shallots and sauté until they are translucent and the gram colours lightly.

Add turmeric and banana blossom and cook for 4–5 minutes until the blossom is tender and cooked.

Increase heat to high and add drumstick leaves with salt. Toss well and cook, stirring constantly until moisture dries up and the leaves wilt.

Sprinkle with grated coconut and serve hot with steamed rice and rasam.

NOTE: To clean the banana blossom, separate each red leaf, pull out the small florets at the base and soak in salted water. The leaves can be discarded. Pull out the stiff pistil of each floret along with the translucent membrane at the base. Drain the salted water and rinse. The florets are ready to use.

KORA BROCCOLI STIR-FRY WITH ASIAN DRESSING

At times something quick and handy is the need of the hour. Asian flavours are my favourite and I am always picking up tips and techniques of Asian cooking. It is not only healthy but also helps to retain all the flavours of the ingredients.

SERVES 4

½ cup kora (foxtail millet, known as kangni in Hindi)
1 tsp sesame oil
1 star anise
1 cup yellow zucchini, diced
1 cup green zucchini, diced
1 cup broccoli florets, blanched
Salt to taste

Dressing

1 tsp sesame oil
1½ tbsp dark soya sauce
1 tbsp garlic, finely chopped
2 tbsps spring onion greens, finely chopped
Black pepper to taste

Bring 2 cups of water to a boil. In a pan, dry-roast the kora on medium–low heat until fragrant. Gradually stir in enough hot water to cover the kora. Reduce the heat and cook until the kora is tender to the bite.

Heat sesame oil on medium–high heat in a wok. When it begins to smoke, add star anise, stir for 2–3 seconds and toss in the zucchini and broccoli. Stir-fry on high heat until the zucchini is slightly tender but still firm. Add salt and toss well.

Add the cooked kora and toss until everything is well combined. Keep aside.

For the dressing, combine all the ingredients in a small mixing bowl and beat well with a fork. Add to the kora and vegetable mixture and toss well. Serve warm.

TIP

Before using it, always wash and soak the grain, then dry again to remove impurities.

SKYU

I was on a trip to McLeodganj when I learnt to make this vegetable and pasta stew, though it belongs to Ladakh in Kashmir. Being taught this recipe was a small comfort, having experienced the big disappointment of missing the Dalai Lama by a few hours. One bowlful of this hearty stew snapped me out of my misery quite effectively. Traditionally, pasta is made with wheat flour, but it's also great made with barley flour or tsampa. The original recipe uses goat's milk, but you can use cow's milk too.

SERVES 4–5

1 cup wholewheat flour
2 tsps oil
1-inch piece of ginger, minced
2–3 garlic cloves, minced
1 large onion, finely chopped
1 large tomato, finely diced
1 large carrot, peeled and sliced
1 potato, peeled and diced
½ cup fresh green peas
½ tsp turmeric powder
½ tsp red chilli powder
½ tsp garam masala powder
4–5 cups vegetable stock or water
Salt to taste
½ cup milk

In a bowl, knead the flour with water to make smooth soft dough. Divide into tiny marble-sized pieces. Roll each piece into a ball and flatten slightly. Then, using your thumb, shape each piece gently into a curved cap to make the pasta. Set them aside.

In a large pan, heat oil on medium heat and sauté ginger and garlic until fragrant. Add onions, sauté until they're translucent, then add vegetables and spices. Sauté for a minute.

Add stock or water, and cover and cook until the vegetables are half cooked, stirring at regular intervals.

Add the pasta and salt and cook until the pasta is tender and rises to the surface. Add milk and simmer for 2 minutes.

Serve hot.

STUFFED TOMATOES IN SWEET BELL PEPPER SAUCE

This dish reminds me of Italy and a meal on Lake Como. It was serendipitous to say the least. The flavours of fresh earthy vegetables with some organic crusty bread and olive oil made for a memorable meal that I am replicating here.

SERVES 4

6 large tomatoes
1 cup mixed bell peppers, finely diced
2 tbsps virgin olive oil
4–5 garlic cloves, minced
½ tsp pepper, freshly crushed

Sauce

1 large onion, sliced
1 cup red bell pepper, pureed
1 cup tomato pulp
1 boiled turnip (optional)
½ cup vegetable stock
½ tsp sea salt
1 tbsp balsamic vinegar
1 tsp chopped fresh oregano
1 tsp chopped fresh parsley
¼ tsp paprika

Wash the tomatoes and slice off the tops and bases so that they can stand. Scoop out the flesh of the tomatoes and keep aside.

In a bowl, mix together bell peppers, 1 tbsp olive oil, garlic and crushed pepper and stuff the tomatoes with this mixture. Set aside.

For the sauce, blend all the ingredients together until smooth.

Gently heat a pan and add the remaining olive oil. Add the blended bell pepper sauce mixture, cover and bring to a simmer.

Arrange the stuffed tomatoes in the sauce, cover and cook for a minute.

Serve hot with salad and bread.

PUMPKIN MOILEE

Pumpkin grows in abundance in India and is available in myriad varieties. While travelling through villages along dusty roads, the sudden sight of bright orange pumpkins growing on thatched roofs of huts make for a picturesque sight indeed! What I like is that the farmer keeps the best pumpkins for his own family; after all, they deserve it. A very versatile vegetable, here I've teamed it with a simple South Indian sauce for a hearty meal.

SERVES 2–3

- 2 tsps coconut oil
- ¾ tsp black mustard seeds
- 1 sprig fresh curry leaves
- 2–3 green chillies
- 1 tsp split white lentils (urad dal)
- 1 tsp split Bengal gram (chana dal)
- 1 large onion, finely sliced
- 1 tsp turmeric powder
- 2 cups diced orange pumpkin, parboiled
- 1 large tomato, finely sliced
- 1 cup vegetable stock
- 1 cup coconut milk
- Salt to taste
- Juice of 1 lime

Heat coconut oil in a large frying pan over medium heat and add mustard seeds, curry leaves and chillies. When they're crackling, add the dals, reduce heat to low and sauté until they turn golden. If the pan gets too hot, remove from the heat for a couple of seconds to prevent the lentils from burning.

Add onion and turmeric and sauté until the onion is translucent. Add the pumpkin and sauté for 5 minutes.

Add tomato, cook for 2 minutes, then pour in the stock and coconut milk and bring to a boil, stirring constantly. Simmer until the sauce thickens and the pumpkin is tender. Remove from the heat and add salt and lime juice.

Serve hot with rotis or brown rice.

CURRIED MUSHROOMS

Walking about in Coorg's markets, one comes across many people of tribal communities selling wild species of mushrooms, locally called kumme. The Kodavas are experts at foraging and kumme are one of the many fascinating ingredients they use in their food. Coorg is also the birthplace of kachampuli, a unique dark vinegar made from the fruit kadampuli or Malabar tamarind. Known as India's version of balsamic, kachampuli is a much stronger variant and drastically reduces cholesterol and blood sugar.

SERVES 4

2 cups button or fresh oyster mushrooms
½ tsp salt
1 tsp coconut oil
1 sprig curry leaves
1-inch piece of fresh ginger, finely chopped
2 onions, finely chopped
½ tsp turmeric powder
2 tsps coriander powder
½ tsp chilli powder
¼ cup coconut milk
½ tsp kachampuli or 1 tbsp balsamic vinegar

Quarter the mushrooms and sprinkle with salt. Toss well and set aside.

Heat coconut oil in a pan on low heat. Add the curry leaves and ginger and sauté until fragrant, then add onions and sauté until they're golden.

Add turmeric, coriander and chilli powders and mix well. Add the mushrooms and stir-fry for a minute before pouring in the coconut milk and kachampuli.

Cook until the sauce coats the mushrooms and remove pan from heat.

Serve hot with rotis.

FENUGREEK PRAWN STIR-FRY

The earthy herby smell of fenugreek wafts through the walls whenever this dish is made at home. It's not a smell I've come to like; however, I love the dish and make it regularly. This is a traditional community recipe and I have always been amazed at how well the bitterish fenugreek complements the juicy prawns.

SERVES 4

- 1½ tsps sesame oil
- 4 garlic cloves, finely chopped
- 1 onion, finely chopped
- 2 green chillies, finely chopped
- 1 tomato, finely chopped
- 1½ cups fresh prawns, rinsed and drained thoroughly
- 1 cup fresh fenugreek leaves, washed and pat-dried
- Salt to taste
- Freshly ground black pepper to taste

Heat the oil in a pan on medium heat, add garlic and sauté until fragrant.

Add the onion, chillies and tomato and sauté until the onion turns golden. Add the remaining ingredients and toss well. Cook for about 3 minutes or until the prawns are cooked and the fenugreek wilts.

Remove from heat and serve hot with rotis.

CHICKEN STEW

Sakru's was a famous café in South Mumbai and every Saturday, on his way home from work, my dad would stop there and bring home this stew. All day, my sister and I would keep asking our nanny what's for dinner, because her answer would evoke giggling fits. She could not pronounce stew and would instead say ishtew, and we found that hilarious! This dish was the café owner's take on Irish stew, and I feel that his addition of chilli, cloves, cinnamon and coriander made it all the more interesting. In my version, I've substituted potatoes and pumpkin with broccoli and mushrooms. Feel free to add cooked kidney beans for a heartier meal.

SERVES 4–6

- 1 tbsp oil
- 1 tbsp minced garlic
- 1 tbsp minced ginger
- 2 large green chillies, slit lengthwise
- 3 cloves
- 2-inch cinnamon stick
- 2 large onions, quartered
- ½ tsp turmeric powder
- 1 large carrot, peeled and diced
- ½ cup diced French beans
- 1 cup broccoli florets
- 1 cup halved button mushrooms
- 1kg curry cut chicken
- 1 cup coconut milk
- 2 cups chicken stock
- Salt to taste
- Freshly ground black pepper to taste
- Freshly chopped parsley, for garnish

Heat oil in a large thick-bottom pot on medium heat. Sauté garlic, ginger, chillies, cloves and cinnamon until fragrant.

Add the onions and sauté until translucent, then add turmeric and vegetables. Sauté for 2–3 minutes.

Add chicken, reduce heat to low and sauté until the chicken begins to brown slightly. Stir in the remaining ingredients, cover the pot and simmer until the stew thickens and the chicken and vegetables are cooked through.

Garnish with fresh parsley and serve hot with bread.

PANCH PHORON YOGHURT MUTTON

Panch phoron is the signature spice mix in Bengali cuisine and a personal favourite because of the burst of spicy, bitter and earthy flavours it lends to a dish. Though mainly used for tempering, I've used it to great effect as a meat rub, encrusting mix and flavouring for pâté. Here, I've powdered it and used it as a marinade, and, I must say, I am pretty pleased with the results.

SERVES 4

- 2 cups fresh yoghurt, whisked
- 1 heaped tsp panch phoron powder (see note)
- 2 tbsps ginger–garlic paste
- 1½ tsps green chilli paste
- ¼ tsp turmeric powder
- ½ tsp cumin powder
- Salt to taste
- 750g mutton leg, cleaned, washed and cut into large pieces
- 1 tbsp mustard oil
- 2 large onions, finely sliced
- 3 cups vegetable or mutton stock, plus more if required

In a bowl, mix together yoghurt, panch phoron powder, ginger–garlic and chilli pastes, turmeric and cumin powders and salt. Whisk well.

Add mutton to the spiced yoghurt and mix well to evenly coat the meat. Cover and set aside for 30 minutes.

Heat mustard oil on medium heat in a large pan. Add the onions and sauté until golden.

Add the mutton with the marinade and cook, stirring continuously for 5–7 minutes until the marinade begins to dry.

Stir in stock, cover and cook for 30–40 minutes or until the mutton is cooked through. Add more stock if required.

When the mutton is cooked, turn off the heat and allow the curry to rest for 5 minutes before serving.

Serve hot with bread or brown rice.

NOTE: To make panch phoron powder, simply grind together a teaspoon each of fennel, nigella, cumin, fenugreek and black or brown mustard seeds to a fine powder in a spice grinder. The remaining powder can be stored in a clean, dry glass jar and used to marinate fish or add to curries.

LENTILS, GRAINS AND BEANS

It is the farmer who provides the food that appears on our tables. But what do you do when there are no farmers and the comfort of the market becomes a distant reality?

The sidelines of forests are where food has been naturally produced for centuries. Organic farms have always been small, family-run units with the produce available in small shops or farmers' markets. It is high time we shift our attention to these markets. One of the best examples of this kind of produce is lentils and beans. Most lentils on our tables come from the fields surrounding the jungles of central India or the hills surrounding the Jim Corbett National Park.

India's love for lentils and beans goes back a long way. Not only are they a great source of plant protein but their soluble fibre is also good for stabilising sugar levels. They are very versatile and can be used in a range of dishes from dals to soups, pâtés, salads and desserts. Soak lentils and beans in stock or water before use so they are easier to make and digest and add a few drops of oil when cooking. Then, let your imagination take over!

COUSCOUS UPMA

There was a café called Shashi in the neighbourhood where I grew up and for years it was my after-school and before-college haunt for steaming hot upma. We often tried to make similar upma at home but somehow never achieved Shashi's perfection. One day though, I mustered enough courage to ask the owner for the recipe and he readily gave it to me. Here, I've recreated the same upma using couscous instead of semolina for a richer flavour and enhanced fibre content.

SERVES 4

1 cup couscous
2 tsps coconut oil
¼ tsp asafoetida
½ tsp mustard seeds
½ tsp urad dal
1 sprig fresh curry leaves
2–3 green chillies, cut into 1-inch pieces
1-inch piece of fresh ginger, grated
1 onion, finely chopped
¼ tsp turmeric powder
½ cup minced carrots
½ cup green peas, boiled
Salt to taste
2–3 cups hot vegetable stock or water
1 tbsp grated fresh coconut

Heat a frying pan on low heat and dry-roast the couscous, stirring continuously until it's pale golden.

In another pan, heat a tsp of oil on medium heat and add asafoetida, mustard seeds, urad dal, curry leaves, chillies and ginger. When the spices are crackling, add onion and sauté until it's translucent.

Add turmeric and immediately mix in the roasted couscous and vegetables. Lower the heat and cook, stirring continuously for 3 minutes.

Mix in salt and gradually pour in the hot stock or water, stirring continuously to prevent lumps. The couscous will swell and begin to absorb the moisture. If all the liquid dries up and the upma looks dry, mix in more liquid. The upma should resemble a very thick slush.

Stir in the remaining coconut oil, cover and cook until all the moisture has been absorbed and some steam accumulates. When done, fluff the upma with a fork.

Garnish with grated coconut and serve hot.

KHAMAN DHOKLA

These savoury steamed split gram cakes define Gujarati cuisine the world over. The nutritional benefits of soaking lentils, grains and nuts have long been known in India, hence, it comes as no surprise that this technique is applied to recipes from across the country. Though dhoklas are now available in many flavours and forms, the traditional recipe still reigns supreme. However, I would like to encourage you try this recipe with different combinations of lentils and beans to derive optimal nutrition.

SERVES 4

- 2 cups split Bengal gram (chana dal), washed well and soaked for 8 hours
- 2–3 large green chillies, crushed to a coarse paste
- 2-inch piece of fresh ginger
- ½ tsp turmeric powder, optional
- ½ tsp soda bicarbonate
- 2 tsps oil, plus as required for greasing cake tin
- Salt to taste
- A few fresh coriander sprigs, finely chopped, for garnish
- 1/3 cup grated coconut, for garnish

Tempering
- 2 tbsps oil
- 1/3 tsp asafoetida
- 2 tsps black mustard seeds

Drain the soaked gram, reserving about half cup of the soaking liquid. Transfer the dal to a mixer or food processor, add chillies and ginger and grind to a slightly coarse paste resembling an oatmeal batter, adding 2 tbsps of water at a time, if required.

Transfer the batter to a large non-reactive airtight container like a glass bowl with a tight-fitting lid or a large plastic jar with a lid. Mix in turmeric if using.

Heat oil in a small pan on low heat and add to the batter along with soda bicarbonate. Mix well, stirring in one direction and cover with lid. Place a weight on the container and set aside in a warm place for up to 6 hours to allow the batter to ferment until it's almost double its original volume.

When the batter has fermented and smells slightly sour, add salt and stir well.

Grease a baking tin liberally and pour in about 3 ladles of batter. Swirl the pan to spread the batter evenly.

Place in a steamer or pressure cooker (without the whistle) and steam for 8–10 minutes, or until the batter is cooked and springy to touch. Remove and cool for a couple of minutes before unmoulding the steamed cake. Repeat with the remaining batter.

For tempering, heat oil in a small pan on medium–low heat until tiny bubbles are visible at the base of the pan. Add asafoetida and mustard seeds and when the mustard crackles, remove the pan. Carefully stir in a tablespoon of water and pour the tempering over each of the steamed cakes.

Garnish with coriander and coconut and cut into large pieces. Serve with tea or chilled buttermilk.

PUY LENTIL AND VEGETABLE BOWL

Puy lentils, known in Hindi as masoor, have a unique peppery flavour and are able to hold their shape during cooking. They are tasty as they are nutritive and very versatile. A rich source of plant protein, these lentils lend beautifully to soups, stews, curries, pilafs and my most favourite, meal bowls.

SERVES 4

1 cup of puy lentils, washed and soaked overnight
1 cup chopped onions
2 garlic cloves, finely chopped
1-inch piece of ginger
½ tsp cumin powder
2 tsps olive oil
Salt to taste
3 cups water
1 cup sliced mushrooms
½ cup chopped tomatoes
2 tbsps finely chopped fresh basil or tulsi
1 green chilli, finely chopped
3–4 large spring onions, sliced
1 large radish, finely chopped
Juice of 1 lime

Drain the lentils, reserving the soaking liquid. In a large saucepan, cook the lentils with onion, garlic, ginger, cumin powder, olive oil and salt for a few minutes, then add water.

Increase heat to medium and bring the water to a boil. Cover the pan partially and stir at regular intervals until the lentils are cooked but firm.

Drain the remaining liquid and discard the ginger. (You can reserve the drained liquid to add to soups or dals.)

Transfer the cooked lentils to a large bowl and add the remaining ingredients except lime juice. Let the vegetables cook in the dal's residual heat.

Add lime juice, toss well and serve immediately.

RED BEANS WITH BUTTERNUT SQUASH

I love beans for the nutty firmness they bring to so many foods. And if there's one invention I'm thankful for when cooking beans, it's the pressure cooker! Without that, dishes like this one would've taken forever to make. Here, red kidney beans are cooked with squash and simple herbs and spices that add just the right amount of flavour without drowning the inherent taste of either.

SERVES 4

½ cup red kidney beans, soaked overnight
3 cups water
2 tbsps olive oil
2-inch cinnamon stick
6 garlic cloves, finely chopped
1 large onion, diced
1 heaped cup diced squash
2 cups vegetable stock
1 tsp red chilli flakes
Sea salt to taste
1 tsp crushed pepper
Fresh coriander sprigs, for garnish

Drain the beans and transfer to a pressure cooker along with water. Let the whistle blow 4 times. When done, allow the pressure to settle before opening the cooker. Drain the beans. (The cooked broth can be reserved to add to soups or dals.)

Heat the oil in a large frying pan and add cinnamon. When it's fragrant, add the garlic and onion and sauté lightly.

Add the squash, stock and chilli flakes. Cook, stirring occasionally, until the pumpkin is tender.

Add the kidney beans to the squash along with salt and pepper. Mix well and cook for another minute.

Garnish with fresh coriander and serve hot with rotis.

LENTILS WITH DRUMSTICKS

As kids, my sister and I enjoyed eating lentils and sucking on drumsticks to get the seeds and pulp out. Back then, had someone told me drumsticks were healthy, I probably wouldn't have eaten them with such delight! Today, though, the story is different. Drumsticks have great nutritional value and brilliant flavour, both of which I enjoy!

SERVES 4

- 2 large drumsticks, peeled and cut into 3-inch pieces
- ¼ tsp salt, plus extra to taste
- 1 cup mung dal, washed and soaked for 10 minutes
- 3 cups vegetable stock
- ½ tsp turmeric powder
- 1 tbsp oil
- ¼ tsp asafoetida
- ¼ tsp mustard seeds
- 2 green chillies, broken into pieces
- 2 sprigs fresh curry leaves
- ½ tsp chopped garlic
- 1 medium onion, finely sliced
- Juice of 1 large lime
- 1 tbsp chopped fresh coriander, for garnish

Place drumsticks in a pan with just enough water to cover, add salt and bring to a boil. Allow drumsticks to boil for 2–3 minutes, then drain.

Drain the dal and transfer to a saucepan along with stock and turmeric. Bring to a boil on high heat before reducing heat to low. Cover partially and simmer for 10 minutes. Stir occasionally.

Cool the dal to room temperature, transfer to a blender and puree until smooth.

In a large pan, heat oil on medium–low heat. Add asafoetida, mustard seeds, chillies, curry leaves and garlic. When the spices are crackling, add onion and sauté until golden brown.

Add drumsticks, pureed dal and salt and simmer for 10 minutes. Add more stock or water if required and cook until the dal is thick and creamy.

Remove from heat, add lime juice and garnish with coriander. Serve hot with boiled red rice.

GREEN BEAN KHICHDI

Common traits among foods across different continents always fascinate me. Take the case of this dish. There's so much in common in terms of technique, ingredients and texture with the Italian risotto or Spanish paella. Of course, risotto is much creamier and starchier, and paella is full of seafood, nevertheless, the similarities are striking. But no matter how much I enjoy risotto and paella, I always crave for khichdi after a long stint away. Here, I've dug into the treasure chest of the variety of beans and lentils available to us and replaced the usual yellow lentils with something special.

SERVES 4–6

1 cup green beans, washed, soaked overnight and drained
4 cups water
2 tbsps vegetable oil
1 tsp cumin seeds
3–4 cloves
1 large onion, finely sliced
¼ cup bean sprouts, washed
1 cup red rice, washed, soaked for 10 minutes and drained
1 green zucchini, finely diced
1 cup finely chopped mixed mushrooms
¼ cup peas
1 small carrot, finely diced
1 tbsp ginger–garlic paste
Salt to taste
½ tsp turmeric powder
1 tsp white pepper powder
2–3 cups vegetable stock or water, simmering

Boil the beans with a tablespoon of oil and water on medium heat until tender.

Heat oil in a large saucepan on medium heat. Add cumin and cloves, and, when they're crackling, add onion and sauté until golden.

Drain the boiled beans and add to the pan with bean sprouts, rice, vegetables, ginger–garlic paste, salt, turmeric and pepper. Sauté until the mixture is fragrant and grains of rice begin sticking to the pan.

Pour hot stock or water, increase heat and bring the khichdi to a boil. When the liquid reduces to the level of rice, reduce heat to low and cover the pan.

Place a griddle on direct flame and the pan with the khichdi on top. Cook until the rice and beans are cooked through and slightly mushy. Stir regularly.

Serve hot with yoghurt.

KIDNEY BEAN CHILLI

Although I don't love spicy food, there are times when I crave something hot like chilli con carne and I quickly head to the meat shop for mince. Once, during Lent, my neighbour sent over kidney bean chilli she'd made to tackle her son's craving for chilli con carne. Fourteen-year-old me was not happy about being given beans instead of meat, but, to my surprise, the kidney bean chilli tasted better than its meatier version. This is definitely for those who crave a dish that will set the mouth on fire.

SERVES 4

1 heaped cup kidney beans, soaked overnight with a pinch of soda bicarbonate
4 cups vegetable stock
1 tbsp olive oil
2 tsps minced garlic
2 large onions, sliced
½ cup red tomato puree
½ tsp freshly ground pepper
1 tsp smoked paprika
1 tsp Tabasco sauce
¼ cup sliced olives
Sea salt to taste
2 tsps finely coriander, finely chopped, for garnish

Drain the beans and rinse well. Transfer to a large saucepan along with vegetable stock and cook, partially covered, on medium heat until cooked through. Stir occasionally.

Heat oil in a large heavy pan on medium heat, add garlic and onions and sauté until fragrant. Add the beans with leftover liquid along with the remaining ingredients.

Cook until the moisture has evaporated and the beans are slightly mashed.

Garnish with chopped coriander and serve hot with a salad and bread of your choice.

OVEN-ROASTED CHICKEN AND VEGETABLES WITH BLACK-EYED BEANS

This is the perfect dish for a large family lunch or dinner when you don't want to complicate things and make too many dishes yet want your guests to be blissfully satisfied. A meal in itself and full of hearty flavours, this dish is sure to bring on a cheerful stupor. If you'd rather have sauce with your chicken, simply puree the vegetables instead of serving them roasted. Add a bit of stock, a touch of butter if you like and simmer for a few minutes.

SERVES 4

Roast chicken and vegetables

- 4 medium chicken legs, scored and soaked in 3 cups brine overnight (see note)
- ½ cup carrots, peeled and cut into large cubes
- 3 large onions, peeled and quartered
- 2 large beetroots, peeled and quartered
- 1 large radish, peeled and chopped
- 1 large garlic bulb, cut in half
- 1 tsp salt
- ½ tsp freshly ground pepper
- 1 tsp freshly ground dried tulsi leaves
- ¼ cup olive oil

Beans

- 2 tsps olive oil
- 1 large onion, finely diced
- 4 garlic cloves, finely chopped
- 1 tsp cumin seeds
- 1 green chilli, finely chopped
- 1 cup black-eyed beans, washed and soaked overnight
- 4 cups vegetable stock
- ½ tsp paprika powder
- Salt to taste
- 1 tbsp finely chopped fresh coriander

Drain the brine and rinse the chicken lightly under running water. In a large bowl, toss all the ingredients for the chicken and vegetable roast together, drizzle with olive oil and set aside for an hour.

Preheat the oven to 150°C on the roast setting. Line a baking tray with lightly greased parchment paper.

Spread the vegetables in an even layer on the tray and place the chicken amidst the vegetables. Roast for an hour, basting the chicken occasionally using the pan drippings from the tray.

For the beans, heat olive oil in a saucepan on medium heat. Add onion and garlic and sauté until the onion is translucent.

Add the cumin, green chilli and beans. Mix well, then add stock, paprika and salt. Simmer, stirring occasionally, until the beans are cooked.

When the beans are done, turn off the heat and add coriander. Mix well and set aside.

Serve the roasted chicken and vegetables hot with warm black-eyed beans.

NOTE: To make the brine, dissolve half cup of salt in 3 cups of water and add 2 cloves, 1 large bay leaf and 2 green cardamom pods. Rest the solution for 20 minutes, then add the scored chicken. Cover and refrigerate overnight.

GRILLED FISH 'N' STEW

One of my first memories of kedgeree is at a Scottish fishing village where I was served the dish topped with a bit of fried fish. The life of a fisherman is arduous to say the least—he sails on dangerous seas to fish delights from their depths. Kedgeree is an Anglo–Indian dish with origins in khichdi, the main difference being the use of fish instead of vegetables. Here, I've substituted rice with barley and added yet another exotic twist.

SERVES 4

- 500g sole fillet, sliced into 4
- 3 tbsps Bengali mustard sauce (kasundi)
- ¼ tsp turmeric powder
- Salt to taste
- 1 tbsp olive oil
- ½ tsp mustard seeds
- 2-inch cinnamon stick
- 1 large onion, finely diced
- 1 cup barley, washed and soaked for 10 minutes
- ½ cup mixed beans, washed, soaked and precooked (optional)
- ½ cup millets, washed and soaked for 10 minutes
- 1 tbsp ginger–garlic paste
- 1 tsp white pepper powder
- 2½ cups vegetable or fish stock, simmering
- 2 tsps chilli oil (optional, see note), for garnish

Brush kasundi on both sides of the fish slices, sprinkle with turmeric and salt and marinate for 10 minutes.

Heat olive oil in a large saucepan on medium heat, add mustard seeds and cinnamon. When the spices are crackling, add onion and sauté until golden.

Add barley, mixed beans, millets, ginger–garlic paste, salt and white pepper. Sauté the mixture until fragrant.

Pour in the stock and bring the mixture to a boil. When the lentils are almost cooked and the moisture has almost dried up, remove and keep aside.

Heat a grill pan on high heat and grill the fish. Halve each slice to get 8 pieces. Flake 4 of the pieces and add to the lentil mixture.

Portion the lentils into serving bowls and top each bowl with the remaining slices of fish.

Drizzle with chilli oil if you prefer spicy food and serve hot with cucumber salad.

NOTE: To make chilli oil, heat 3 tbsps of oil in a pan then remove from heat. Add 1 tbsp of chilli powder or chilli flakes. Allow the oil to cool completely and transfer to a jar.

LAMB SHANKS WITH CURRIED LENTILS

This dish has been one of my favorites since I first developed it for a restaurant I helmed. It was one of the popular dishes, but I continued to experiment with it and build on ideas. The original dish was a spicy South American delight, but the recipe I finally fell in love with is this one, enhanced by the robust flavours of South India.

SERVES 4

Lamb

½ tbsp cumin seeds
½ tbsp fennel seeds
8 garlic cloves, finely sliced
2 green chillies, finely sliced
2 tbsps tamarind pulp
4 large lamb shanks
Salt to taste
2 cups split pigeon peas, washed and soaked for 15 minutes
8 cups vegetable or mutton stock
1 tsp coconut oil
1 heaped tbsp Madras curry powder
Salt to taste
½ cup coconut milk

Quinoa

1 cup red quinoa
2 cups stock
Sea salt to taste
1 tsp finely chopped fresh herb of your choice

Pear salad

2 large pears, diced
1 tbsp lemon juice
2 tbsps mayonnaise
¼ tsp mustard paste
Edible flowers, for garnish

For the lamb, blend cumin and fennel seeds, garlic, chillies and tamarind pulp in a blender to a smooth paste. Transfer to a large mixing bowl.

Add the lamb shanks and salt and toss well, rubbing the marinade into the lamb. Cover and set aside for an hour.

Meanwhile, add lentils, stock, coconut oil and curry powder to a large saucepan and bring to a boil on high heat. Then reduce heat to low, add the lamb shanks and partially cover the pan.

Cook until the lamb is cooked through and the lentils are slightly mushy. Add salt and coconut milk and cover and cook for 5 more minutes.

Toast quinoa in a pan on low heat for 5–7 minutes until it's light to touch. Stir in stock, salt and herbs and cook until the moisture is absorbed and the quinoa is tender.

Prepare the pear salad by tossing all the ingredients together in a bowl. Garnish with edible flowers.

Serve the lamb shanks hot with quinoa and pear salad on the side.

BREADS AND BAKES

We are witnessing new forms of organic farming today, from terrace farming in urban areas to the production of microgreens using coconut husks as soil. The current rage of aquaponics and hydroponics and other ways of growing produce have changed the ecosystem of farming.

From the health and nutrition perspective, organic food is known to contain 50 per cent more nutrients, vitamins and minerals compared to chemically grown food. One way of incorporating the goodness of organic food into our meals is through breads and baked foods, thanks to the variety of ingredients available to us. Not only are they wholesome fillers with our meals, but they can be tantalising in taste too.

Spiced Ragi Roti

Guliappam

Bati

Bajra Roti

Poee

Thepla

Mixed Lentil and Millet Dosa

Anglo–Indian Vegetable Bake

Baked Brinjal

Baked Mackerel in Lemon Salt

SPICED RAGI ROTI

Ragi is one of the healthiest and most mineral-rich grains available to us. A rich source of iron, it produces a large amount of heat in the body, making this roti perfect for the cold winters of North India. You can still enjoy it if you live in a warm place; just make sure you pair it with buttermilk.

SERVES 4

1 cup ragi flour
1 large onion, finely chopped
1 large green chilli, finely chopped
2 tsps finely chopped fresh curry leaves
Salt to taste
Warm water as needed
Oil to toast

In a mixing bowl, combine ragi flour with onion, chilli, curry leaves and salt. Then, gradually knead the flour with small amounts of water to make a soft dough. Cover the dough with a damp kitchen towel and allow to rest for 15 minutes.

Divide the dough into 4 equal portions and roll each into a ball. Place each ball on a lightly greased plate and flatten it into a patty. Keep patting it into a thin disc, turning the plate as you do so, until the roti is about ¼-inch thick. Repeat with the other balls.

Heat a griddle on low heat and drizzle evenly with oil. Carefully place a roti on the griddle and toast both sides, gently pressing it down with a flat spoon. Cook for a few seconds until the surface looks bubbly, then flip it over and cook the other side until dark spots appear on the surface. Repeat with the other rotis.

Serve hot with curried mushrooms (page 112) or lentils with drumsticks (page 130).

GULIAPPAM

There are as many types of appams in South India as there are varieties of lentils and beans. This one is my favourite, with its crisp surface and soft interior. The only special equipment required is the guliappam pan, but, if you don't have one, try using the same batter to make baby dosas or pancakes. You will not be disappointed!

SERVES 4–5

- 1 cup split pigeon peas (arhar dal)
- ½ cup mung dal
- ½ cup puy lentils (masoor dal)
- 1 tsp turmeric powder
- 2 green chillies
- 2-inch piece of ginger
- Salt to taste
- Oil for shallow-frying

Combine the lentils in a large mixing bowl and wash properly. Soak overnight in 5 cups of water.

Next day, drain the water, reserving about half a cup. Transfer the lentils with the reserved liquid to a grinder, add turmeric, chillies and ginger, and grind to a thick coarse batter, the consistency of cooked oatmeal.

Transfer batter to an airtight container and set aside in a warm place. Place a weight on the container and allow the batter to ferment for 6–8 hours.

Add salt to the batter and mix well. Lightly grease the guliappam mould and heat on medium–high heat until hot.

Add ¼ tsp oil to each mould and 1 tbsp of batter. Cover the mould and reduce heat to low. Allow the appams to cook for a minute, then flip each piece over. Cook for 30–45 seconds more.

Serve hot with chutney, raita or dal of your choice.

BATI

Bati baking on hot coal is a common sight in the markets of Rajasthan, Uttar Pradesh and Bihar, where these breads are made. The deftness with which the women knead the dough, shape the batis and bake them without using tongs to flip them is a mesmerising sight. I learned to make bati from a lady in Pushkar. I walked away with a new skill and left her with a funny story to tell her grandkids, thanks to all the hopping about every time I burned my fingers on red-hot coals.

SERVES 4

2 cups wholewheat flour
¾ cup water, or as required
3 tbsps oil
Salt to taste
½ tsp carom seeds

Mix all the ingredients together to form a stiff dough. Cover with a damp cloth and allow to rest for 15–20 minutes.

Preheat the oven to 180°C.

Divide the dough into 8 portions and roll each into a ball or bati. Place them on a greased baking tray and bake for 20–25 minutes until the batis are cooked through and golden.

Serve hot with kidney bean chilli (page 134). Bati can also be served as a bread roll with any soup.

BAJRA ROTI

A simple unparalleled joy among the fanciest foods is eating hot bajra rotis brushed with freshly churned white butter. A common millet found in the humblest of kitchens across India, bajra is also one of the healthiest and easiest-to-digest foods. Here, I've added a touch of fenugreek to offset the slightly rough flavour of bajra.

SERVES 4

- 2 cups bajra flour
- 1 tbsp dried fenugreek leaves (kasuri methi)
- ½ tsp salt
- 1 cup warm water
- 2 tbsps of oil

Sift the flour into a bowl, add fenugreek leaves and salt and mix well. Add water gradually to knead into a soft smooth dough.

Divide the dough into 6 portions. Place each portion on a dusted rolling board or kitchen counter and roll into discs about 6 inches in diameter.

Heat a griddle on low heat, and cook each roti for 30–45 seconds on each side until golden and cooked through and small dark spots appear on the surface.

Place each roti directly on a flame for a few seconds and flip using a pair of tongs. Transfer to a plate and immediately brush with clarified butter.

Serve hot with curry or dal of your choice.

POEE

The tinkle of bicycle bells in rural Goa is what one wakes up to early in the morning, with freshly baked poee delivered to your doorstep. Devouring them hot with tea as the village comes to life is how most Goans start their day. The addition of bran provides a good dose of fibre, which keeps one comfortably satiated until lunchtime.

SERVES 4–6

1 heaped cup wholewheat flour
2 tsps fresh yeast
¾ cup lukewarm water
A pinch of sugar
½ tsp salt
¼ cup milk
2 tbsps bran

Sift the flour on a clean kitchen counter.

In a bowl, stir yeast with water and sugar to dissolve slightly. Cover the bowl and set aside in a warm place for about 10 minutes to allow the yeast to bloom.

When the yeast mixture gets frothy, add it to the flour and knead into a soft pliable dough. Cover with a damp kitchen towel and set aside in a warm area to proof (rise).

When the dough has risen to double its volume, add the salt and knead it lightly.

Divide into large lime-sized portions and roll into balls. Brush them with milk and dust generously with bran. Place on a greased and dusted baking tray and set aside to allow the bread to rise a second time.

Preheat oven to 225°C.

When the bread rolls are double in volume, bake them for 10–15 minutes or until the bread is golden brown.

Remove from the oven and transfer the poee to a cooling rack. Cool thoroughly before eating.

THEPLA

Gujarat's favourite go-to bread for any occasion, thepla, are now available pan-India like dosa. For many years, I was under the impression that thepla were only flavoured with fenugreek, because I only saw methi thepla everywhere. It was only when my best friend's mother served me thepla flavoured with dill, coriander, spinach, red spinach and even spring onion greens over several visits that I realised how versatile this humble bread is! This recipe is for methi thepla, but feel free to experiment with all kinds of greens until you find your own favourite.

SERVES 4–6

- 1 cup finely chopped fresh fenugreek leaves
- ½ tsp turmeric powder
- 1 tsp red chilli powder
- ½ tsp cumin–coriander powder in equal proportions
- ½ tsp carom seeds
- Salt to taste
- ¾ cup chickpea flour (besan)
- 1½ cups wholewheat flour, plus extra for dusting
- Oil, as required

In a bowl, mix together fenugreek leaves with the spices, carom and salt. Set aside for 15–20 minutes to allow the spices to draw out moisture from the fenugreek.

Mix chickpea flour with the spiced fenugreek, then slowly add wholewheat flour to knead into a smooth soft dough. Add 1 tbsp of oil, knead well, cover with a damp kitchen towel and set aside.

Divide the dough into lime-sized portions. Shape each portion into a ball and flatten between your palms. Dust with flour and, using a rolling pin, make 6-inch-diameter discs. Repeat for remaining portions.

Heat a griddle on medium–low heat. When hot, place the thepla on it, reduce the heat and cook until small bubbles appear on the surface. Drizzle very little oil around the edges and brush some more on the thepla.

Turn it over and cook the other side until done, brushing with very little oil and pressing along the edges to ensure even cooking. When the thepla is fragrant and small brown spots appear on the surface, remove from the griddle. Repeat with remaining discs. Serve hot with chilli jam.

MIXED LENTIL AND MILLET DOSA

It's amusing how so many people associate the dosa with rice. Yes, the most common recipe includes a batter of rice and split black lentils, but dosa batter is not limited to just that. You could try any number and combination of lentils, millets and other grains to make your own signature dosa. Here's mine. I hope you like it.

SERVES 4

1 cup foxtail millet
¼ cup split green gram (green mung dal)
¼ cup split pigeon peas (arhar dal)
¼ cup split Bengal gram (chana dal)
¼ cup split black lentils (urad dal)
¼ tsp asafoetida
½ tsp cumin seeds
1 cup almond milk
Oil, as required

Mix together millets, lentils, asafoetida and cumin seeds. Transfer small batches to a mixer and grind into a fine flour. (This can be stored for future use.)

When ready to make the dosas, whisk the flour with almond milk to make a thick, smooth and easily pourable batter. Set aside for 30 minutes.

Heat a non-stick pan and drizzle lightly with oil. Swirl it around so the oil spreads across the pan.

Pour a ladle of batter on the hot pan and spread it into a thin pancake. Cook for 30–40 seconds until the edges begin to curl and turn golden brown. Carefully flip the dosa and cook the other side for another 6–8 seconds.

Serve hot with chutney of your choice.

ANGLO–INDIAN VEGETABLE BAKE

For Mum, no party was considered complete without a bake. Come party time, this bake was my signature. The crusty topping and cheese truly make it tantalising. The British left behind a legacy of baking and one-pot cooking, which the Anglo–Indians continue to do justice to. This dish, though sans cheese, is temptingly delicious for any event.

SERVES 4

Sauce

1 cup cauliflower florets, boiled
½ cup almond or coconut milk
1 tbsp tapioca flour
1 cup vegetable stock

Filling

2 tsps olive oil
4 garlic cloves, crushed
1 large onion, finely chopped
1 large yellow zucchini, diced
1 large green zucchini, diced
3 large carrots, peeled, diced and blanched
1 cup broccoli florets, blanched
12 Italian sun-dried tomatoes, quartered
2 spring onions, finely sliced
1 fresh rosemary or thyme sprig
Salt to taste
Freshly ground black pepper to taste
½ tsp paprika
1 tbsp vinegar

For the sauce, blend all the ingredients except stock in a blender into a smooth paste. Transfer to a pan. Add vegetable stock and simmer on medium heat until it thickens slightly. Set aside.

Preheat oven to 150°C.

For the filling, heat oil in a pan on medium heat, add garlic and onion and sauté until the onion turns translucent. Add zucchini, carrots and broccoli and sauté until the zucchini are tender.

Add all remaining ingredients, toss well and remove from the heat.

Add the sauce and toss until the vegetables are evenly coated.

Transfer the vegetables to a baking dish and bake for 30 minutes. Serve hot.

BAKED BRINJAL

Baingan bharta used to make an appearance on our table once a week. My favourite part of the cooking process is the charring of the brinjal directly over the flame. That fragrance makes me hungry. Another favourite dish was thinly sliced brinjals sprinkled with salt, chilli powder and salad oil and baked in the oven with loads of cheese on it. Here, I've replaced the cheese with an equally satisfying hung curd sauce.

SERVES 4

- 4 long brinjals, finely sliced lengthwise
- 1 tsp Himalayan salt or sea salt
- ½ tsp pepper
- 1 tsp smoked paprika
- ¼ cup olive oil

Sauce

- 1 cup hung curd
- 1 tsp cumin powder
- 1 tsp coriander powder
- 1 tbsp tahini
- 1 tsp chilli–garlic paste (see note)
- Finely grated rind of 1 lemon
- ½ cup fresh coriander leaves

Lightly score the brinjal slices and soak them in cold salted water for an hour.

Drain the water and rinse the brinjal slices properly. Sprinkle with salt, pepper and paprika, add olive oil and toss well. Set aside for 10 minutes.

Preheat the oven at 150°C.

Layer the slices on a lightly greased baking tray and bake for 20 minutes.

For the sauce, add all the ingredients to a mixing bowl, setting aside a few coriander leaves for garnish. Whisk well, cover and set aside for 20 minutes to allow the flavours to merge.

When the brinjal slices are cooked through, divide equally between four plates, drizzle liberally with the sauce and serve hot with lemon wedges on the side.

NOTE: Grind 2 green chillies with 4 large garlic cloves to make a smooth chilli–garlic paste. Refrigerate to use at any time.

BAKED MACKEREL IN LEMON SALT

In Hampstead, I worked in a Japanese restaurant for a while, and this dish was taught to me by the chef. As chefs, we often try to complicate dishes with too many ingredients. The best dishes I've enjoyed have been the simplest ones with minimal ingredients. A dish where you can actually taste the ingredients without them being masked in sauces and spice is truly joyful. Here, I've used lemon salt to lend a unique flavour to the fish.

SERVES 4

4 mackerel (200g each)
1 tbsp olive oil
2 tbsps lemon salt (see note)
2 tbsps lime juice
½ tsp red chilli paste
½ tsp turmeric powder
2 tbsps fresh coriander, finely chopped

Place the fish in a bowl of iced water for 10–15 minutes. Drain.

Using a filleting knife, fillet the fish, removing the head and bones. Keep the skin intact.

Preheat the oven to 200°C.

Lightly drizzle a pan with olive oil and heat on low heat. Starting with skin side down, pan-fry the fish for 2 minutes on each side. Transfer to a baking tray.

In a bowl, mix together lemon salt, lime juice, chilli paste and turmeric powder and brush both sides of the fish lightly but evenly with the mixture. Bake for 5–7 minutes.

When done, carefully transfer fish to serving plates and garnish with coriander. Serve hot with a salad and soup of your choice.

NOTE: Lemon salt is available in most supermarkets, however, you can easily make your own. Simply mix a cupful of sea salt with 1½ tbsps of lemon rind. Toss well and store in a clean dry airtight glass jar. Allow to mature for a week before using.

BEVERAGES

One is often in a dilemma about having a drink when out. Different kinds of alcohol affect the body differently. Wines are the safest bet when out, especially dry wines as they regulate blood flow and, red wines, which are great for the heart.

Fruits and vegetables are great in drinks, but it is important to check the fruits diabetics are allowed to have. Another important thing to remember is to drink fruit-based beverages immediately to get the maximum nutrition out of them. Unsweetened tea and coffee and vegetable juices are the best. If you want to be adventurous sometimes, a mixologist can create some great concoctions.

Flavoured waters are also great thirst-quenchers and source of hydration. Herbs or fruits soaked in water for a few hours lend their essence to water.

Here are some refreshing beverages that are simple to put together and so delicious, you'll never want to go back to sugary cocktails or mocktails again!

PEANUT BUTTER SMOOTHIE

Two common beverages many diabetics miss are milkshakes and smoothies, given the high sugar content in both. However, with a few simple substitutions, anyone can enjoy a healthy milkshake or smoothie without it affecting sugar levels. This smoothie is a case in point. Feel free to experiment with coconut milk, cashew milk or soya milk.

SERVES 1

1 ½ cups almond milk (see note)
2–3 dates, pitted
2–3 drops vanilla essence
2 tbsps unsweetened peanut butter
1 apple, peeled and chopped
5–6 ice cubes

Pour almond milk into a blender jar and add the remaining ingredients. Allow the dates and apple to soak for 10–15 minutes, then blend into a smoothie.

Pour over ice in a tall glass and serve immediately.

NOTE: To make your own almond milk, soak a cup of almonds overnight in 2 cups of water. Next morning, drain and reserve the soaking liquid, peel the almonds and transfer them to a blender. Add some soaking water and blend into a smooth paste. Strain the paste through a cheesecloth, squeezing out as much milk as you can. Do not discard the remnants of the blended almonds. They're great for gluten-free pie and tart shells.

CARROT CORIANDER JUICE

Many people frown at the thought of carrot juice. My mother would too, calling it insipid, although she'd quietly drink the prescribed glassful every week. She liked carrots in salads, and it made me wonder why she didn't like the juice. One day, she forced me to taste some. When blended with water, carrots tend to take on a slightly bitter flavour and lose their sweetness. The best way to counter that is by adding coriander, ginger and cinnamon.

SERVES 2

6 large carrots, peeled and roughly chopped
½ cup fresh coriander with stalks, roughly chopped
½ tsp coriander seeds
2-inch piece of fresh turmeric
1-inch piece of ginger
1 cup water
¼ tsp cinnamon powder
Rind and juice of 1 lime
8–10 ice cubes

In a blender, blend all the ingredients together except ice and lime juice, until well combined and almost smooth. Strain through a fine strainer.

Pour over ice into small glasses.

Stir in lime juice and serve immediately.

EARTHY HOT CHOCOLATE

Who doesn't love a good hot chocolate, especially on a cold wintry day? Dark chocolate is good for diabetics and a wonderful comfort beverage, but, in most cases, comes heavily sweetened. Here, I've used Dutch cocoa for depth of flavour.

SERVES 2

- 2 tbsps Dutch cocoa
- 2 cups almond milk or coconut milk
- ½ tsp vanilla essence or Angostura bitters
- ¼ tsp cinnamon powder
- 2 tbsps maple syrup
- ¼ tsp sea salt

Mix all ingredients together in a pan and bring to a simmer on medium heat.

Stir with a whisk to make sure the mixture is smooth.

Serve hot.

SPINACH AND APPLE SMOOTHIE

This can well serve as a dessert in liquid form! The flavours of apple pie come together with just the right amount of tartness from the apple cider vinegar to give you a refreshing summer drink.

SERVES 1

2 large apples
½ cup spinach leaves, chopped
¼ tsp cinnamon powder
2 tbsps chia seeds, soaked
1 tbsp apple cider vinegar
1 tbsp lemon juice
1 tbsp maple syrup (optional)

Wash the apples and spinach thoroughly in salted water.

Blend all the ingredients together in a blender until smooth. Drink immediately.

PEAR AND ALMOND MILK SMOOTHIE

When I was young, we would get all our vegetables and fruits from vendors who came to our doorstep, carrying produce in large wicker baskets balanced on their heads. Seasonal fruits were brought by special vendors and my favourite time of the year was when the first pears would show up. Back then, when Bombay's winter evenings felt almost cool, I'd cajole my nanny to make me pear crumble. Today, though, I prefer to use them for this chilled smoothie.

SERVES 2

2 large pears
½ cup almond milk
¼ tsp cinnamon powder
¼ tsp Angostura bitters
A few cubes of ice

Wash the pears properly, peel and chop roughly.

Blend all the ingredients together in a blender. Pour over ice in a tall glass and serve chilled.

MIXED BERRY LASSI

In the garden next door, there was a mulberry bush and, come summertime, we would spend all day picking ripe mulberries and staining our clothes in the process. Those were the days! Here is a simple smoothie that brings back all those fun memories.

SERVES 1

1 cup mixed berries
½ cup Greek yoghurt, chilled
¼ tsp black pepper
¼ tsp vanilla essence
¼ tsp turmeric powder

Wash the berries properly and transfer to a blender.

Add the remaining ingredients and blend until smooth.

Chill in the refrigerator for an hour before serving.

CHUKKU KAAPI

My earliest memory of coffee is being allowed one sip from my father's cup every morning. Dad was from South India and very particular about how coffee was prepared. His cuppa was always flavoured with cardamom and, growing up, this became an addiction for me. Later, when I went to London to study, I worked at a bar where the master barman taught me how to flavour coffees, transforming them from stimulating beverages to memorable experiences. This spiced coffee is one of the many delicious recipes that I share with you.

SERVES 4

4 cups water
1½ tbsps jaggery (or 2 tablets of sweetener)
1 tbsp dry ginger powder
1 tsp black pepper powder
1 tbsp coffee, freshly ground
1 tsp cumin seeds
4 green cardamom pods
20 tulsi leaves (holy basil)
A pinch of salt

Add water and jaggery or sweetener to a saucepan and bring to a boil. When jaggery dissolves, add all the ingredients except tulsi and salt and boil for about 4 minutes.

Add tulsi, reduce heat to low and simmer for 2–3 minutes. Add salt and turn off the heat.

Strain the coffee into serving cups and serve hot.

SPICED TEA

This is a great herbal remedy for lowering sugar levels, as well as great as flavouring for dessert bases. Black tea has polysaccharides that prevent sugar from being absorbed into the bloodstream. The only thing one needs to remember is to never boil tea, only steep it to bring out its flavour.

SERVES 2

2½ cups water
1-inch cinnamon stick
2–3 black peppercorns
1 tulsi sprig
1-inch piece of ginger
4 fresh mint sprigs
Grated rind of 1 lime
1 tsp dehydrated hibiscus petals
1 tsp black tea leaves

Add all the ingredients except tea to a pan and bring to a simmer on medium heat. Simmer for 5 minutes.

Add tea leaves to a teapot and pour the hot spiced water into it. Steep for 3 minutes and strain into cups. Serve hot.

FLAVOURED WATER

One of the most popular beverages in my restaurant was served free, even to those who weren't dining in. In fact, many people visited the restaurant just to enjoy a cool glass of our flavoured water. We played around with oranges, pineapples, lemongrass, mint and coriander. But you are free to try many more ingredients.

SERVES 4

1 pear
1 orange
1 lemon
1 tsp fennel seeds, lightly crushed
1-inch piece of ginger, julienned
2 cloves, lightly crushed
1-inch piece of fresh turmeric
1 litre water
¼ cup lemon juice
1 cup ice cubes

Wash and finely slice the fruits and add to a jug.

Add the remaining ingredients except lime juice and ice. Allow to macerate for 20–30 minutes.

To serve, pour into glasses over ice and add lime juice. Alternately, you could mix everything together and refrigerate the jug, topping up with more water as it gets consumed.

GINGER LEMON SHERBET

Walk the beaches of Bombay and you invariably have a 'golawallah' who will sell you a variety of coloured syrups poured over shaved ice to make lip-smacking ice candy. The rotating wheel that shaves the ice, the drizzling of the syrup and the golawallah's deft fingers adding touches of lime, ginger and salt still make for a fascinating sight. But now, I get a bit apprehensive about enjoying those beachside treats. I prefer to make them in the safety of my own kitchen and enjoy a tall jugful during the hot summer months.

SERVES 2

- ¼ cup freshly extracted ginger juice
- ¼ cup lime juice
- ¼ tsp cardamom powder
- 1 litre chilled water
- A few drops of sweetener, if required
- Ice cubes, as preferred

In a large jug, mix together ginger juice, lime juice and cardamom powder.

Top up with chilled water and add a few drops of sweetener if required. Rest the sherbet for 5–7 minutes to allow the flavours to merge.

Pour over ice in glasses and serve immediately.

DESSERTS

For a chef who began his career specialising in French patisserie, I thought this would be the hardest chapter to put together, given my natural attraction to cream and sugar. But it was surprisingly easy! Not only did this chapter challenge the chef within me to think, but it also gave me the opportunity to look at Indian desserts in a new light.

So many of our desserts use vegetables, flowers and even lentils. All I needed to do was tweak some ingredients and play a bit more with flavours and the ideas started to roll. Please treat these recipes as templates; as your sugar levels begin to reduce and you're allowed a wider variety of fruits and vegetables, feel free to substitute ingredients to create your own unique desserts.

An important thing to remember is portion size. Here, I've kept the portion sizes small—I've seen this simple measure making a huge difference in keeping sugar levels in check. If you control your diet and make a few small but significant changes, diabetes really can't stop you from enjoying life.

Just take a bit of care and life will be sweet again.

JAMUN SORBET

The java plum or jamun appears in the late summer months. As kids, my sister and I would spread a clean bedsheet under the jamun tree and throw sticks at the branches to make the fruits fall off. The sheet would catch the fruit and after having our fill, we'd quietly put it to wash, hoping Mum wouldn't notice. But she always did, thanks to the telltale purple stains. This was before she was told jamun helps to control blood sugar levels. Today, she enjoys the fruit as much as we did.

SERVES 4–6

1kg fresh jamun, deseeded
1 cup honey
½ tsp black salt
½ tsp black pepper powder
2 tsps lemon juice
1 tsp chaat masala

Puree the jamun and strain the pulp through a sieve. Transfer to a food processor.

Add honey, black salt, pepper powder, lemon juice and chaat masala and blend well together.

Transfer to small bowls or popsicle moulds and freeze overnight.

Serve chilled.

HEALTH BARS

I love spending time in national parks and Satpura is one of my favourites. The landscape is unlike that of any other jungle and it's the only national park where they allow a small walking safari or a lovely canoe ride. The walking safari is very exciting but also quite draining, especially on hot days when you suddenly feel exhausted. Whether you're on a safari or an evening walk, I recommend carrying these bars. They come in handy to combat hunger pangs, crazy cravings and sudden loss of energy.

SERVES 1

- ½ cup steel-cut oats
- ⅓ cup flax seeds
- ½ cup almonds (or any other nuts)
- ¼ cup basil seeds or chia seeds
- ½ cup fresh dates, pitted and minced
- ½ cup mixed dried berries, finely chopped
- ½ cup dessicated coconut (optional)
- 1 tsp cocoa powder, for dusting

Heat a pan on medium–low heat and toast the oats, flax seeds, almonds and basil or chia seeds until the almonds colour slightly.

Transfer the mixture to a grinder and grind into a coarse or fine powder depending on the texture of your preference.

Transfer the dates and berries to the same pan and add a teaspoon of water. Cook on low heat until the water evaporates, and the dates and berries are mashed into a coarse paste and turn off the heat.

Add the powdered mixture and stir well. Spread out on a lightly greased board or plate and roll or press evenly. Allow to cool.

Cut into cubes of desired size. Dust with cocoa powder to prevent moisture from setting in.

TIP

These health bars can keep up to a week without refrigeration and up to two weeks if refrigerated.

PLUM FOOL

This is one of the first dishes I learned to make during my pre-teen forays into the kitchen. In those days, there was no limit on the amount of sugar or cream we could eat, so this dish was a decadent seasonal treat to welcome the monsoon. In fact, leftover Plum Fool made breakfast the next day even more delicious because it paired perfectly with hot toast. Here, I've played with the flavours a bit and added an Asian touch. And though I've cut down on the richness, the magic of the dish is intact.

SERVES 4

4 large plums, pitted and sliced
1 cup freshly brewed light tea
2 sticks lemongrass
2 cloves
2 cups hung yoghurt
¼ tsp cardamom powder
2 tbsps chopped nuts, for garnish
¼ tsp clove powder, for garnish

In a thick pan, combine the sliced plums with tea. Crush the lemongrass using the handle of a knife and add to the pan along with cloves.

Cook the plums on medium heat until they turn into a rough pulpy mash. Remove pan from the heat and allow to cool.

Whisk together yoghurt and cardamom powder until smooth.

To serve, add a dollop each of the plum mash and yoghurt in a bowl and swirl lightly. Garnish with nuts and a sprinkle of clove powder. Serve warm or chilled.

QUINOA OATS PUDDING

Quinoa, popular today as a superfood, has been sacred to the Aztecs for several centuries. Legend has it that the honour of harvesting the first grains of quinoa was reserved for the king or leader of the tribe. A filling grain, quinoa always tastes better when it's slightly toasted in a warm oven or pan, cutting out any bitterness as well. This dessert is easy to make and also works great for breakfast.

SERVES 3 TO 4

½ cup white quinoa
½ cup rolled oats
½ cup boiled barley
1 cup unsweetened apple juice
1 cup almond milk
½ tsp cinnamon powder
6 prunes, cut into slivers
3 tbsps slivered almonds, lightly roasted
Few stalks of wheatgrass, chopped
2 tbsps dried cranberries or blueberries

Heat a pan and lightly toast the oats and quinoa till they feel light to the hand.

Gradually, add apple juice, almond milk and cinnamon and cook, stirring continuously until the quinoa and oats swell.

Add the barley. If required, stir in half a cup of water.

Add the prunes and mix well.

Portion the pudding into bowls. Garnish with almonds, wheatgrass and berries and serve warm.

SIGNAL STOP FIGS

For a long time, figs for me were synonymous with traffic signals. In my childhood, we never saw figs in the local market. You could only buy fresh figs at traffic lights where families walked to waiting cars and sold the fruit after brief bouts of bargaining. The inclusion of this recipe may surprise many as figs are not seen as diabetic-friendly, but if you enjoy a fresh fig once in a while, it will do no harm. The sugar level is much lower than in a dried fig and the fibre content much higher.

SERVES 4

4 fresh figs
½ cup red wine
1 tsp balsamic vinegar
A few drops of Angostura bitters
1-inch cinnamon stick
2–3 cloves
4 small rosemary sprigs

Wash and score the figs into quarters, taking care not to cut them through.

Preheat oven to 150°C.

Whisk together wine, vinegar, bitters and spices in a mixing bowl. Add the figs and, using a teaspoon, drizzle the wine marinade over the cut portions. Set aside for 10–15 minutes.

Transfer the figs to a lightly greased baking tray. Place a rosemary sprig in each fig and drizzle with marinade. Bake for 7–8 minutes or until tender.

Serve warm.

JUST BANANAS

When Mum was diagnosed with diabetes and was allowed only bananas, we went into overdrive, concocting banana treats for her. There were banana fritters for tea and flambéed bananas for fancy dessert; mashed bananas spread on toast for breakfast and mashed bananas dusted with cinnamon or cocoa and rolled in buttermilk pancakes for brunch. Here, I'm sharing the first treat I had made for her.

SERVES 4

4 large ripe bananas
¼ cup desiccated coconut
½ cup unsweetened coconut milk
¼ tsp vanilla essence
¼ tsp cinnamon powder

Preheat the oven to 180°C.

Slice the bananas lengthwise into halves. Arrange them in a baking dish and add the remaining ingredients on top.

Bake for 10 minutes or until the bananas are tender.

Serve warm.

BLACK RICE COCONUT PUDDING WITH BAKED PEARS

A black rice kheer made by a friend from north-east India inspired this dish. I loved the nutty flavour and texture of black rice and also the hints of lemongrass infused in the coconut milk in the original version. However, I'm not a great fan of kheer, and so, I've tried making my own version, playing with my favourite spices and adding fruit. I would have loved to caramelise the pears but baking them brought out a beautiful natural sweetness, which prevented me from experimenting further with this recipe.

SERVES 4

1 cup black rice, washed and soaked for an hour
2 cups water
¾ cup coconut milk
¼ tsp Angostura bitters
1 tbsp lemongrass juice (see note)
2 large pears
¼ tsp cinnamon powder
2 tbsps coconut slivers, toasted
2 tbsps almond slivers
Edible flowers (optional)

In a pan, bring rice and water to a boil on medium heat. Cook, stirring occasionally, until the rice is cooked but firm, and moisture has almost completely evaporated.

Add the coconut milk, bitters and lemongrass juice. Mix well and turn off the heat. Keep warm.

Preheat oven to 150°C.

Peel and slice the pears or cut into halves lengthwise and scoop out the seeds. Place them, cut side down, on a greased and lined baking tray, dust them with cinnamon powder and bake for 8 minutes, until they turn soft and golden brown.

Arrange pears cut side up on serving plates. Spoon the black rice pudding on them. Garnish with coconut and almond slivers and edible flowers and serve hot.

You could also chill the pears and pudding separately and serve the dessert chilled.

NOTE: For lemongrass juice, crush a large stalk of fresh lemongrass with 2 tsps of water using a mortar and pestle. Strain through a cheesecloth tied in a bundle and squeeze well to get the juice.

CHIA PANNA COTTA WITH FROZEN BERRIES

We always create desserts with love and passion. Chia seeds are similar to tulsi seeds, extremely healthy and nutritious. They're used frequently during hot summer months for its cooling effects on the body.

SERVES 4

Panna cotta

½ cup chia seeds
1¾ cups almond milk (see page 166)
¼ tsp Angostura bitters or vanilla essence
2 gelatin leaves

Dark chocolate truffle

100g dark chocolate
½ cup thick coconut milk
¼ tsp cinnamon powder

Garnish

Mint sprigs
2 cups frozen berries

For the pudding, soak the chia seeds in a bowl in half a cup of water for 15 minutes, then drain. Transfer to a pan and cook with the almond milk and Angostura bitters.

Soften the gelatin in a little warm water and add to the chia mixture. Allow to cool.

For the truffle, grate the chocolate into a pan and add coconut milk and cinnamon. Gently heat the mixture until the chocolate has melted. Set aside.

Wash and rinse, but do not wipe, six shot glasses or bowls.

When the truffle has almost cooled, pour a layer into the glasses and leave to set.

Next, add the chia mix on top of the truffle in each glass and allow to set.

Garnish with frozen berries or mint and serve.

SPICES AND HERBS

ALLSPICE (*PIMENTA DIOICA*)

This pea-sized fruit native to West Indies has the flavour and aroma that are a blend of cinnamon, nutmeg, peppercorns and cloves. It is used whole in pickles, gravies and meat preparations. In powder form, it is added to baked products like biscuits and Christmas puddings and relishes and pickles.

AMCHUR (DRY MANGO POWDER)

This tangy ingredient is basically sun-dried green mangoes in powder form. Rich in vitamin C, amchur is used to add a touch of sourness to a dish. It needs to be kept dry in storage as it can get lumpy due to moisture.

ANISE (*PIMPINELLA ANISUM*)

This spice is common in seed form, but, in powder form, it is used in fish soups, sauces, rye bread, coffee, cakes, cookies and candies. It is the main ingredient in the manufacture of the liqueur anisette.

ASAFOETIDA (*FERULA ASAFOETIDA*) HING

This spice is native to Afghanistan, and the Afghans cook it whole as a vegetable. But the main ingredient is the sap, which is dried and ground to a powder. With an onion-like flavour, it is used mainly in lentil dishes and other vegetarian food.

BASIL (*OCIMUM BASILICUM*)

This herb has many variants, from tulsi to the cinnamon-flavoured basil, European and Thai basil. It's one ingredient that uplifts many a dish. Mixing it up with kitchen herbs like marjoram, turmeric, oregano and rosemary provides a great remedy for various illnesses. Basil is especially good for diabetics.

BAY LAUREL (*LAURUS NOBILIS*) TEJ PATTA

Belonging to the avocado family, this leaf has its origins in Asia Minor and the Mediterranean. It contains an important and volatile oil, cineol. Fresh leaves are bitter and the dried ones, if unused for too long, lose their potency. The evergreen tree grows to a height of 20m. Its aromatic leaf is widely used in pickling, stews, soups, vinegars and curries.

CARAWAY (*CARUM CARVI*) SHAHI JEERA

These are the dried fruits of a biennial plant native to northern Europe and widely used on breads and in pork, liver and kidney-based dishes. Caraway is also the main ingredient of the liqueur kümmel.

CARDAMOM (*ELETTARIA CARDAMOMUM*) ELAICHI

This seed belongs to the ginger family. Cardamom is extremely popular in the Middle East, where it is infused in coffee. The seed is widely used in Indian cuisines as it has a sharp but pleasant flavour. In the Orient, it is a popular breath freshener. Cardamom is a common flavouring agent in rice, vegetables and baked dishes. Its oil is used in perfumes and liqueurs.

CHILLIES/CAPSICUM/BELL PEPPERS (*CAPSICUM GENUS*) MIRCHI/SHIMLA MIRCH

Chilli, like salt and pepper, is a universal spice that has transformed world cuisine. It is used extensively in Latin America, Asia, Africa and the Caribbean and in certain Oriental cuisines. Paprika, a mild cousin, comes from the frutescens variety of chilli, and is used mainly for the colour it imparts to food. Used in powder form, the membrane and seeds are mixed in. It's used as seasoning in biscuits, gravies and sauces.

CINNAMON (*CINNAMOMUM VERUM*) DALCHINI

Known to aid in weight loss and lowering blood sugar, cinnamon spice is the dried bark of the tree, which is an unusual feature among spice plants. Cinnamon and cassia are among the oldest spices known to humankind. The difference between the two is slight with cinnamon being better in flavour and intensity. True cinnamon has tightly rolled quills and is thinner than cassia. It is native to South India, Sri Lanka, Seychelles, Madagascar and the West Indies. Medicinally, cinnamon is used as a stimulant and a digestive. Cassia is cultivated in China, Indonesia and Vietnam. It is less intense in flavour than cinnamon.

CLOVE (*EUGENIA CARYOPHYLLUS*) LAUNG

The clove tree is evergreen, and it originally grew in abundance in the Moluccas or Spice Islands. On flowering, they're covered in tiny red blossoms, which are dried in the sun. Cloves are rich in essential oils like eugenol, used in the manufacture of soaps, perfumes and toothpastes. It is an important spice in Indian masalas.

CORIANDER (*CORIANDRUM SATIVUM*) DHANIA

A perennial herb, the Americans know coriander as cilantro. The leaves and stems have a pungent flavour, while the dried seeds are sweet and aromatic with a hint of bitterness. It is one of the principal spices for seasoning fish and meat.

CUMIN (*CUMINUM CYMINUM*) JEERA

Black cumin is grown and cultivated primarily in Iran, the Middle East and Kashmir. Cumin seed is pale brown when dried and, like fennel and aniseed, it has a warm and slightly bitter taste. In Indian cuisine, cumin is an important ingredient in meat dishes and ground masalas. In the coastal areas, it is widely used in fish preparations. Cumin is known to lower blood sugar levels.

CURRY LEAVES (*MURRAYA KOENIGII*) CURRY PATTA

This plant belongs to the basil family as well and grows wild in India. Its leaves lend a pungent and aromatic flavour to dishes. The curry leaf is widely used in Indian and Asian cooking.

CURRY POWDER

A unique blend of spices used predominantly in Indian cuisine, curry powder is mainly added to curries and sauces for an enhanced flavour.

DILL (*ANETHUM GRAVEOLENS*)

Dill is also consumed as a vegetable in India besides being a wonderful herb. It is great for diabetics and has 70 components that help to fight diabetes. Widely used by apothecaries, dill originated in the Middle East and made its way to kitchens in Russia and Europe where it is widely used.

FENNEL (*FOENICULUM VULGARE*)

Fennel or saunf is widely used in Arabian and Indian cooking. Its medicinal properties are well known. Fennel is used in several infusions, including certain teas. Anethole, one of the phytochemicals found in fennel, is anti-inflammatory and helps to fight cancer.

GARLIC (*ALLIUM SATIVUM*) LASUN

Garlic is an essential ingredient in most cuisines for its pungent and aromatic flavour. There are various types of garlic, the most common being the white variety. Pink or purple garlic is fleshier. Indispensable to Asian and Mediterranean cooking, garlic is strongest in its raw state, taking on sweeter and milder notes when cooked. As it burns, it lends a bitter taste. Garlic also enhances the flavours of other ingredients. It aids in lowering blood sugar—many cultures encourage people to eat a garlic clove every day.

GINGER (*ZINGIBER OFFICINALE*) ADRAK

Ginger is the tuberous root of the plant. It evolved in Southeast Asia and today, India is the largest exporter of fresh, dried, ground and, preserved ginger. The spice is closely associated with good health. The Chinese and Indians have long used ginger medicinally. It is widely used in chutneys, pickles, stewed fruit, pies, curries and cakes. The essential oil oleoresin is obtained from ginger. It fights diabetes, high blood lipids, cholesterol and high triglycerides.

MACE/NUTMEG (*MYRISTICA FRAGRANS*) JAVITRI/JAIPHAL

Nutmeg is unique in that its fruit gives two distinct flavours. Rich in vitamin A, mace is scarlet in colour and a rich red-brown when dried. It is the outer covering of the seed. Commercially, mace and nutmeg are used in sauces and confectionery. However, both must always be used in minute quantities.

MINT (*MENTHA*) PUDINA

Mint goes well with lamb, fruit-based desserts and cooling beverages. Spearmint (*Mentha spicata*), which has slender delicate leaves is preferred over peppermint (*Menthe piperata*) in cooking. Mint compliments aubergines and tomatoes. It is also a relaxant and helps lower blood sugar; however, those with acid reflux should avoid mint.

PEPPER (*PIPER NIGRUM*) KALI MIRCH

Indigenous to the Malabar coast of southwest India, pepper has its origins in the Western Ghats and is one of the most widely used spices in the world. The term pepper comes from the Sanskrit word pippali, meaning berry. Medicinally, pepper is a stimulant and digestive, but is more in vogue as a seasoning. The spice is an important ingredient in curing Virginia-style hams, and in the making of pastrami. In India, it is essential to the preparation of rasam (pepper water). Pepper's pungency is due to alkaloids, which, together with a volatile oil, constitute the sensory qualities of pepper.

ROSEMARY (*SALVIA ROSMARINUS*)

Used in tonnes of dishes, rosemary is key to flavouring meats and stews. Rosmarinus officinalis is a heart tonic, and the herb is also useful to treat metabolic syndrome. Rosemary's most active phytochemical, carnosol, lowers oxidative stress. This wonder herb is an anti-inflammatory agent and great for fighting diabetes and cancer too.

SAGE (*SALVIA OFFICINALIS*)

Light and velvety to touch, sage's strong flavour is key to many a dish and cuisine. Its medicinal properties are also wonderful. Sage contains polyphenols and its rosmarinic acid content is higher than rosemary itself. Besides being effective against diabetes, sage is also used to treat patients with Alzheimer's.

SESAME SEEDS (*SESAMUM INDICUM*) TIL

These seeds have a nutty flavour and are used essentially in vegetarian dishes in Indian cuisine, and sprinkled on Indian breads as a topping. The seeds are black or white, the oil comprising half the seed weight. In the US, this seed is widely used in cooking, lighting and lubrication.

STAR ANISE (*ILLICIUM VERUM*) CHAKRI PHOOL/BADIYAN

Brought to India by Chinese traders centuries ago, star anise is also known as Chinese anise. The name badiyan is of Persian origin. The spice is derived from an evergreen Chinese shrub of the magnolia family. Used extensively in Asian cuisine, this spice's flavour is a combination of liquorice and aniseed. Shaped like a star, its tiny seed in the centre is light brown and shiny. In India, star anise is widely used in Goan and Chettinad cuisine and is a main ingredient in spice powder mixes for its aromatic and health properties. One star added to stock or rice dishes lends a rich gamey flavour.

STEVIA (*STEVIA REBAUDIANA*)

Stevia is the new herb on the block. Its natural sweetness is several times that of sugar. One leaf is enough at times.

THYME (*THYMUS VULGARIS*)

Thyme is used a lot in European cooking. It has 75 active phytochemicals that work against diabetes and it's also anti-inflammatory.

TURMERIC (*CURCUMA LONGA*) HALDI

Native to India, China, Java and Peru, this plant is a member of the ginger family. The mature roots of the plant are boiled, peeled and dried, then ground into a fine powder. Turmeric contains a yellow pigment called cur cumin and is used as a cloth dye in Asia. Also used in cosmetics and medicines, its main use is in food. Turmeric is occasionally substituted as a cheaper version of saffron although it has a different taste. The spice gives a warm, pleasant flavour with a hint of bitterness. It also plays an important role in the religious and marital customs of South Asia.

GLOSSARY

A

Atta: Flour

B

Bake: To cook by dry heat, usually in an oven.

Bake blind: Partially or fully bake a pie crust or shell. The pastry is lined with foil and filled with beans before baking to prevent it from rising.

Baking powder: A raising agent. Baked dishes containing baking powder should be allowed to stand for a few minutes, allowing the leavening agents to work before being cooked in the oven.

Bangra/Bangda: Mackerel

Barbecue: A loosely defined method of grilling over coal.

Baste or mop: To moisten food with a liquid while cooking. This keeps the meat or other foods from drying out and brings out colour and flavour. A spoon, brush, bulb baster or miniature mop can be used.

Blanch: To plunge food briefly in boiling water and then in cold water to stop the cooking process. Blanching is used to loosen skins of fruits and vegetables, or to prepare them for further cooking by another method. Not to be confused with parboiling.

Blanching/peeling tomatoes: Score the top and bottom of the tomatoes with a sharp knife. Plunge into boiling water for a minute. Remove and place in cold water. Peel off the skin.

Bran: It is the coarse outer layer of most cereal grains, which is removed during the early stages of milling. It is the best-known source of dietary fibre.

Braise: A method in which food is first browned and then cooked in a tightly covered pan or oven with a small amount of liquid. It is cooked at low heat for a long period of time.

Breadcrumbs: The crumbs from dried bread. Toast bread in an oven (do not brown it) then crush it.

Broth: A flavourful liquid made by simmering meat, poultry or seafood in water. Broths and stocks are virtually the same thing. The word 'stock' simply implies that it is being saved (stocked) for another preparation, such as a sauce or soup. Broth should stand on its own and be ready to serve.

Brown stock: A broth made by browning the main ingredients (usually meat, meat bones or poultry) on a stove or in an oven before adding liquid.

C

Caramelisation: All meat and vegetables contain some sugar in the form of carbohydrates. Under intense dry heat, as in roasting or sautéing, these sugars break down. The result is a brown colour and rich flavour called caramelisation.

Cereals: They consist of edible grass seeds. The cultivation of cereals marked a transition from hunting to agriculture.

Chapati: Native to India with a long history, it is a fine example of primitive bread, which is unleavened. Indigenous to different continents, such as the Ethiopian injera and Mexican tortillas, it is a dietary staple. Broken and used as a spoon to scoop up gravies, it is made with atta and originally ground with a mortar and pestle.

Chiffonade: Literally, this means 'made of rags'. It refers to thin strips of vegetables and herbs. Several leaves are staked on top of each other and rolled tightly like a cigar. Thin slices are made across the leaves while holding the roll tightly.

Chop: There are four separate chopping dimensions, from rough chop (any large and regular sizes), to coarse chop, chop and, the smallest, mince.

Condiment: An aromatic mix such as pickles, chutneys and sauces and relishes that accompanies food. Usually kept on the table throughout the meal service.

D

Dal: Lentils

Deep-fry: To immerse food completely into hot fat at 140°C–190°C.

Dice: There are at least four different dicing sizes: brunoise (⅛" x ⅛"); concasse (¼" x ¼"); medium dice (⅓" x ⅓"); and large dice (¾" x ¾").

Double boiler: A larger pan with water at the bottom, and a smaller pan placed above the water. The water is the bottom pan is simmered, warming or cooking the ingredients in the smaller pan. A glass double boiler is highly recommended, for the obvious reason that one can then tell when to add more water.

Dredge: To coat food lightly with flour, cornmeal or breadcrumbs to enhance browning or deep-frying.

F

Fold: To combine one mixture with another through repeated gentle turning-over motions—not beating or stirring—to keep the air in.

G

Ghee: Clarified butter.

Glazing: This term has two meanings. One is subjecting a roast of meat to high heat and basting it until a glistening, golden brown crust is formed. The meat glaze is purely a stock, which has been reduced to a glutinous consistency. With the proper infusion of cream or butter, a glaze can be used as a sauce. Second, glazing can also mean coating pastries and cakes with icing.

Grate: Cut foods such as cheese or cabbage into shreds, flakes or tiny particles using a tool with sharp-edged holes, a knife or a food processor.

Grilling: Using a grill. There are two kinds of grilling techniques, direct and indirect. Direct cooking is grilling without the lid, and directly over a fire. This is usually used for large pieces of meat, chicken or vegetables, and imparts a tasty caramelisation. The fire itself can be very hot on one side, and cooler on the other. Indirect grilling, as its name implies, grills, or more properly, bakes on the opposite side of the grill where there's no coal. Smoking is a variation of the indirect grilling process.

H

Herb/spice: A herb is the leafy portion of an aromatic plant. A spice is practically every other part of that plant, i.e., the bark, root, etc.

I

Incorporate: To mix thoroughly.

Infusion: A hot liquid steeped with herbs and flavourings like spices and peels. The extraction of flavour from a food in a hot liquid (below the boiling point) is also an infusion. Usually refers to teas and coffees but can also apply to cooking.

J

Jaggery: Unrefined sugar, also known as gur.

Joint: Cutting of game and poultry along the joints.

Julienne: Foods that are cut into 1/16" x 1/16" x 1½" – 2" strips, or vegetables cut into thin matchstick-sized strips.

K

Kakdi: Cucumber
Kanda: Onion
Kanji: Also conjee, this is boiled rice water.
Khus khus: Poppy seeds
Kolbi: Prawn

L

Liaison: Binding or thickening of soup or sauce by means of egg yolk, blood or starch such as flour (see roux), arrowroot, cornstarch or tapioca.
Limboo/Nimboo/Nimbu: Lemon or lime

M

Macaroni: A form of pasta widely liked in the Indian subcontinent.
Macerate: To soak ingredients in a liquid, usually alcohol (maceration usually applies to fruits) or a flavoured liquid. When a saline solution is added, maceration occurs, the purpose of which is to draw out water.
Marinade: A liquid including seasonings and acid (vinegar, citrus or wine) in which food is steeped before cooking in order to flavour it. Marinating does not actually make the meat tender. To do so would seriously alter the texture of the meat and make it unpleasant. Food marinated with cornflour should have oil added in to avoid sticking in a lump.
Marinate: This is the most popular method for tenderising meat using a variety of ingredients and allowing flavours to marry for certain lengths of time.
Masala: A powdered mix of spices or herbs. There are two types of masalas—dry and wet. Traditionally, all masalas are hand-pounded and hand-ground.
Millet: Used for brewing and eating since prehistoric times in Asia, Africa and Europe. It travelled from Europe to Arabia, the Persian Gulf and to India, where it has been grown since 2000 BC, and to China following the Silk Route.
Mise en place: Literally, this means 'put in place'. It requires one to thoroughly read the recipe and organise all the ingredients, equipment and serving pieces prior to cooking.

N

Non-reactive: In cooking, any non-porous material that won't react (by discolouring or changing the taste) with acidic foods. This includes glass, stainless steel, glazed ceramic and enamel.

O

Oxidation: A chemical reaction that occurs when a substance is exposed to oxygen. The oxygen reacts with elements in the substance to change it, like when cut apples turn brown.

P

Pounding: A method practised for years. Done to break down connective meat tissues and release the juices. These juices must be retained in the meat with the help of flour, or much flavour is lost.
Pan-frying: To pan-fry, one treats food more gently as opposed to sautéing. Pan-frying occurs when one uses about ¼ inch of fat or oil and cooks on moderate to moderate–high heat. It leaves the food relatively undisturbed, except for an occasional flip or turn with a spatula, fork or tongs. Good for large pieces of food and those coated with bread before cooking, such as thick pork chops, bone-in chicken and whole trout. Fats with a high smoking point like vegetable oil or lard are traditional for pan-frying.

Parboil: Partial cooking of food in boiling or simmering liquid. Similar to blanching, but the cooking time is longer.
Phoolgobi: Cauliflower
Piercing: Foods which have skin like apples, potatoes or tomatoes need piercing when being baked whole.
Pith: The soft, white membrane that lies between the peel and pulp of a citrus fruit. It has a bitter flavour, and, when trying to extract the zest, one avoids using the pith.
Poach: To cook food gently in hot liquid just below the boiling point. Liquids can vary from broths, to water and syrups.
Prepared vegetables: Vegetables that are cut, chopped or grated as specified in a recipe.

R

Reduce: To boil a liquid until its volume is reduced by evaporation. This thickens the liquid and intensifies the flavours. So, season a reduction after it is made, not before.
Refresh: To submerge cooked food in cold water to cool it quickly and stop further cooking. It is also known as shocking.
Reheating: Foods being reheated must be steaming and hot to the touch.
Resting: Heat drives meat juices from the surface when cooking. Allowing meat to rest before slicing lets these juices seep back towards the surface.
Roast: Roasting in India is usually done in a pan. It's cooking proteins using moist or dry heat from all sides.
Roti: Indian flatbread

S

Shakkar: Sugar
Salt: Namak. Add salt in the final stage or after cooking as it draws moisture out of foods. It is sodium chloride, irrespective of its origins from the sea or a mine. The crystals come in different shapes and have some differences. How they act and react with various foods becomes a matter of importance to cooking. Onion salt is a combination of freshly chopped onion and salt. This is then dried and bottled. Onion salt gives a mild onion flavour to dishes like salads.
Seal: To fry meat over high heat, thus, preventing the juices from escaping.
Shenga: Drumsticks, also known as *sujjan ka phalli* or *sengad.*
Simmer: To cook food just below boiling point.
Sauté: In French, sauté means, 'to jump'. This describes the method of cooking in which food is cooked quickly in a small amount of butter or oil. The food 'jumps' as it is either rapidly stirred or shaken over heat (see pan-fry and stir-fry). To sauté, one uses only the smallest amount of fat or oil—enough to lightly coat the bottom of the pan and prevent the food from sticking. It is done on moderate–high to high heat, hot enough to make the food sizzle, sputter and even jump a little the instant it hits the pan. Keep the food in constant motion by stirring with a spoon or actually flipping the pan, so that it browns evenly. Choose fast-cooking foods for sautéing, such as cutlets, vegetables or shrimp. Use fats such as clarified butter, vegetable oil or a mix of butter and oil.
Scald: To heat milk almost to the boiling point, until tiny bubbles begin to form around the inside edge of the pan.
Score: Make shallow or deep cuts in a decorative pattern with a sharp knife. Ham fat is often scored in diamond shapes. You score the thickest part of whole fish with 2–3 slashes so that part will cook as fast as the thin areas.
Seasoning: Salt and pepper
Shred: Cut or grate into long, even, thin strands.

Sooji/suji/rawa: Semolina

Soup: Soups in India are usually shorbas.

Soy sauce: This extremely important ingredient in Asian cooking is a dark, salty sauce made by fermenting boiled soybeans and roasted wheat or barley. Although there is essentially one main type of soy sauce, China and Japan produce a number of varieties ranging in colour from light to dark and in texture from thin to very thick.

Steam: Cook on a rack placed above boiling liquid but never touching, in a covered container.

Steep: Soak a food item such as tea, herbal leaves or saffron in liquid that is just under boiling point to soften the food or flavour the liquid.

Stew: Cook food slowly in a simmering, well-seasoned liquid in a covered pan.

Stir-fry: Sautéing small, uniform pieces of food quickly on high heat, often in a wok or skillet, tossing the food constantly.

Stirring: Stir food from outside in to ensure even heating. Cooking time and food quantity should be in proportion. When cooking large portions of food, stir the food at short intervals to allow even cooking.

Stock: A more or less gelatinous and aromatic liquid prepared by poaching meat, fish or bones in water or more stock. Virtually, the same as broth or bouillon, the only difference is that these terms imply the liquid will be served as is, whereas, stock implies eventual use in another preparation. (See broth, brown stock, white stock.)

Strain: Place food in a sieve to separate liquid from solids or force a soft food through a sieve to purée it and remove hard particles.

T

Tamarind: Fruit of a tall shade tree native to Asia and North Africa. The large brown pods contain small seeds and a sweet–sour pulp. This pulp is a common flavouring in Indian and Middle Eastern cuisines. Used like lemon juice.

Tamatar: Tomato

Tava: A griddle or cast-iron flat pan for roasting spices and chapattis.

Tel: Oil

Temper: To slowly add a hot liquid to eggs or other foods to gradually raise their temperature without making them curdle.

Tempering: With reference to Indian cooking, tempering or tadka refers to cooking spices in oil before or after a dish is prepared. When done after, it is poured hot over the cooked food.

Tomato purée: Tomatoes that have been briefly cooked and strained. Used as a thickener.

V

Vanilla: Grown extensively in South India especially in Munnar and Cochin.

Vinegar: A souring agent used extensively in Indian cooking. There are different types of vinegars—rice vinegar from the south, kadampuli and toddy vinegar from the coastal areas, sugarcane vinegar from the north.

W

Wheat: As with other cereals, milling influences wheat's nutritive value. Originating in the Valley of the Tigris around 7000 BC, it spread to Asia Minor, Egypt and Europe. Ancient Middle Eastern civilisations used wheat as a staple grain, especially for porridge. Wheat germ is the husk, which is removed during milling. Ten grams of husk produces two grams of fibre.

Whisk: To beat to mix using a whisk.

Y

Yoghurt or *curd:* Yoghurt is made by inoculating partially evaporated milk with a fermenting bacterium, which thickens the milk.

Yeast: There are many fungi, some good and some bad. The ones which interest us are better known as sugar fungi. This is mainly due to their ability to digest glucose and produce alcohol, carbon dioxide and energy.

Z

Zeera: Cumin

Zest: The outer skin of citrus fruits where the essential oils are concentrated. The French word is zeste, not to be confused with ziste, the white pith beneath the outer layer of skin.

TABLE OF MEASURES

1 cup = 250ml	1 tbsp = 3 tsp	1 tsp = 5ml

CONVERSIONS

Fahrenheit to Centigrade: Subtract 32, multiply by 5, divide by 9.
Centigrade to Fahrenheit: Multiply by 9, divide by 5, add 32.

OVEN TEMPERATURES

Fahrenheit	Celsius	Description	Fahrenheit	Celsius	Description
225	110	Cool	250	120	Cool
275	140	Very low	300	150	Very low
325	170	Moderate	350	180	Moderate
375	190	Hot	400	200	Hot
425	220	Hot	450	230	Very hot

Meat	Style	Temp (F)	(C)	Time Per 450g	
Beef	Rare	140		60	20 minutes
	Medium	160		71	25 minutes
	Well done	170		76	35 minutes
Veal	Well done	170	76	35 minutes	
Lamb	Medium	170	76	35 minutes	
	Well done	182	83	40 minutes	
Mutton	Medium	170	76	40 minutes	
Pork	Well done	185	85	35 minutes	
Cured Ham	Well done	150	65	30 minutes	

OVEN TEMPERATURES FOR ROASTING MEAT AND POULTRY

	(F)	(C)	
Beef, mutton and pork	325	162	
Lamb and veal	300	162	
Chicken 4–5kg	350	176	2 hours
Duck 5–6kg	350	176	2–3 hours
Goose 10–12kg	325	162	3–4 hours
Turkey 10–13kg	300	148	3–4 hours
Turkey 14–17kg	275	135	6–8 hours

ABOUT THE AUTHOR

Chef Michael Swamy is a pioneer in the area of food media and is a chef, food stylist, food writer and travel photographer based in Mumbai, India. A graduate of the prestigious Le Cordon Bleu, London, he has conceptualised and handled major food shows. He has authored *The East Indian Kitchen*, *Masala Dabba* and *Easy Guide to Pairing Indian Food with Wine* and has won the Gourmand Award several times. As chef patron and creator of several restaurant brands, he has set a benchmark for Indo–French, Indo–Portuguese and Indo–Spanish cooking.

His work with Pugdundee Safaris as well as with boutique resorts like Te Aroha in Dhanachuli, Uttarakhand, has helped him create a niche market for himself.

He is associated with a few leading hospitality universities like WGSHA Manipal and Symbiosis Pune, where he teaches and sets up courses on food media.

Encountering diabetes closer to home and having to ensure many meals for his mother as well as clients coming to his restaurants inspired him to take another look at his own diet and health and rediscover as well as create recipes that could provide optimal nutrition and taste too.
www.michaelswamy.com